Navigating Heart's Turmoil

Understanding Relationship Anxiety, Its Causes, and Steps to Find Balance and Connection

Isabelle Thornley

Summary

Chapter 1: The Heart's Terrain: An Introduction to Relationship Anxiety

Love, connections, and relationships are the basic building blocks of human existence. They shape our lives, influence our decisions, and often define our happiness. However, not all relationships are filled with sunshine and bliss. Some navigate through stormy seas and encounter uncertain territory. This is where relationship anxiety comes into play – a misunderstood yet prevalent condition in the realm of human interactions. In this chapter, we will embark on a journey through the heart's terrain, exploring the depths of relationship anxiety and its impact on our lives.

Unveiling Relationship Anxiety

At some point in our lives, many of us have experienced relationship anxiety. It's that lingering feeling of unease, doubt, and fear that creeps into our minds when we begin to intertwine our lives with another. Its intensity may vary, but the impact it has on our emotional and mental state is profound. Relationship anxiety encompasses a range of concerns, including fear of abandonment, doubts about compatibility, insecurities about one's worthiness of love, or even a general fear of commitment.

The Origins of Relationship Anxiety

To truly understand relationship anxiety, it is essential to explore its roots. For many individuals, relationship anxiety stems from past experiences, trauma, or unhealthy patterns in past relationships. These experiences shape our perception and make it difficult to trust and feel secure in present relationships. However, it's also important to recognize that relationship anxiety can arise in individuals without any prior traumatic experiences. It can manifest due to personal insecurities or even societal pressures to conform to certain relationship norms.

The Impact on Mental Health

Relationship anxiety can take a significant toll on an individual's mental health. It can give rise to a constant state of worry, anxiety attacks, or even full-blown panic disorders. Uncertainty in a relationship can lead to obsessive thoughts, over-analysis of every interaction, and a constant need for reassurance. Moreover, relationship anxiety often spills over into other areas of life, affecting productivity, self-esteem, and overall emotional well-being.

Understanding Attachment Styles

Attachment styles play a pivotal role in relationship anxiety. Developed in early childhood and influenced by our primary caregivers, these attachment styles dictate how we connect with others. Secure attachment provides a strong foundation for healthy relationships, while anxious and avoidant attachment styles contribute to relationship anxiety. Recognizing our attachment style and how it shapes our behaviors can be immensely valuable in understanding and addressing relationship anxiety.

Managing Relationship Anxiety

The good news is that relationship anxiety can be managed and even overcome with the right tools and techniques. Building self-awareness, exploring past traumas or experiences, and challenging distorted beliefs can be instrumental in alleviating relationship anxiety. Additionally, open and honest communication with a partner, relationship therapy, or support groups can provide the necessary guidance and reassurance to navigate the uncertain terrain of relationships.

The Role of Self-Care

Self-care is a fundamental aspect of managing relationship anxiety and fostering healthy relationships. Practicing self-compassion, setting boundaries, and prioritizing one's emotional well-being can create a solid foundation for sustainable connections. Taking care of oneself allows individuals to approach relationships from a place of security and authenticity, reducing the grip of anxiety and allowing love to flourish.

Navigating the Challenges

Relationship anxiety is not without its challenges. It requires dedication, patience, and understanding. It's important to remember that healing relationship anxiety is not an overnight process and that setbacks may occur along the way. However, with a commitment to self-growth and embracing vulnerability, individuals can find solace in healthy connections.

Acknowledging Diverse Experiences

It is crucial to acknowledge that relationship anxiety is a complex issue with diverse experiences. Everyone's journey through the heart's terrain will be different, influenced by their unique background, cultural context, and personal inclinations. However, by shedding light on relationship anxiety, we can cultivate empathy, understanding, and a supportive environment for those grappling with this heartfelt struggle.

Heart's Quivers: What is Relationship Anxiety?

In matters of the heart, anxiety can be an overwhelming force that casts a shadow on even the most promising relationships. While it is normal to feel a certain level of unease and uncertainty in any romantic partnership, some people experience intense relationship anxiety that can be debilitating and hinder the growth of their emotional connection. These individuals often find themselves caught in a web of questions and doubt, second-guessing their choices and fearing the worst outcomes. In this chapter, we will explore the intricacies of relationship anxiety, its origins, symptoms, and potential ways to address and overcome its grasp on our hearts.

Understanding Relationship Anxiety:

Relationship anxiety refers to the persistent worry and fear experienced in romantic relationships. It is characterized by an overwhelming need for reassurance, constant doubt about one's partner's love and commitment, and an incessant desire to protect oneself from potential heartbreak. This anxiety can stem from a variety of factors, including past relationship experiences, childhood experiences, or personal insecurities. It is important to note that relationship anxiety can affect individuals regardless of gender, age, or relationship status.

Origins of Relationship Anxiety:

The roots of relationship anxiety can often be traced back to early life experiences and significant relationships. Childhood experiences, such as inconsistent parenting or witnessing unstable relationships, can shape an individual's perception of love and intimacy. These experiences may lead to a deep-seated fear of abandonment or an inherent belief that love can never truly be relied upon. Additionally, past traumatic relationship experiences, such as infidelity or betrayal, can create lasting emotional scars that contribute to relationship anxiety.

Symptoms of Relationship Anxiety:

Relationship anxiety manifests itself in various ways, and its symptoms may differ from person to person. Some common symptoms include:

1. Excessive need for reassurance: Individuals with relationship anxiety may constantly seek reassurance from their partners, fearing that their love is not reciprocated or that their relationship is on the verge of ending. They may repeatedly seek validation and become emotionally dependent on their partner's affirmations.

2. Fear of abandonment: Those experiencing relationship anxiety often live in a perpetual fear of being abandoned by their partner. This fear may manifest as clinginess, possessiveness, or an inability to tolerate any distance or alone time within the relationship.

3. Incessant doubt and intrusive thoughts: The anxious mind frequently bombards the individual with irrational thoughts and scenarios, leading to a constant state of doubt. They may obsessively question their partner's feelings or engage in endless "what if" scenarios, envisioning potential relationship threats.

4. Hypervigilance and constant monitoring: Individuals with relationship anxiety become hyper-aware of their partner's behavior and may resort to constant monitoring of their actions, seeking any signs of potential trouble or disloyalty. This hypervigilance can lead to unnecessary conflict and strain the relationship.

Coping with Relationship Anxiety:

Overcoming relationship anxiety requires a combination of self-reflection, open communication with your partner, and, in some cases, professional help. Here are some strategies that can help you cope with relationship anxiety:

1. Self-reflection and introspection: Take the time to understand the root causes of your relationship anxiety. Reflect on your past experiences and how they may be shaping your current fears. Journaling, therapy, or seeking the guidance of a trusted confidante can aid in this self-exploration.

2. Open and honest communication: Share your fears and anxieties with your partner in an open and honest manner. Letting them in on your internal struggles can strengthen your bond and create a safe space for dialogue. Together, you can work on developing strategies that foster a greater sense of security and trust.

3. Challenge irrational thoughts: Recognize that not every fearful

thought you experience is grounded in reality. Challenge your anxious thoughts by asking yourself if there is evidence to support them. Practice replacing negative thoughts with more constructive and positive ones.

4. Set healthy boundaries: Establish boundaries within the relationship that enable you to nurture your individuality and personal space. Allow for independent activities and interests, understanding that healthy relationships thrive when both partners have room to grow and develop.

5. Mindfulness and self-care: Engage in practices that promote self-care and mindfulness, such as meditation or engaging in hobbies you enjoy. Taking care of your emotional well-being can help alleviate anxiety and reduce the impact on your relationship.

6. Seek professional help if needed: In cases where relationship anxiety significantly impacts your daily life and relationship, seeking professional assistance from therapists or relationship counselors can be immensely beneficial. They can provide guidance, support, and practical strategies tailored to your specific needs.

Relationship anxiety can be a formidable foe to overcome, but with self-reflection, open communication, and proactive coping strategies, it is possible to find greater peace and security within your romantic partnerships. By addressing the origins of your anxieties, challenging irrational thoughts, and taking care of your mental well-being, you can create a foundation for a healthier and more fulfilling relationship. Remember, relationship anxiety may be a part of your journey, but it does not have to define the destination.

The Origins of Unease: Historical Perspectives on Relationship Anxiety.

In modern society, it is commonplace to experience relationship anxiety—a feeling of unease or distress regarding the stability, commitment, or overall satisfaction of one's romantic partnership. While this phenomenon is well-documented in contemporary psychology and relationship sciences, its historical origins have often been overlooked. In this chapter, we aim to explore the historical perspectives on relationship anxiety, shedding light on the factors that contributed to its emergence, evolution, and impact on human relationships throughout different periods.

Primitive Societies: Insecurity Amidst Uncertainty

In the distant past, humans lived in primitive societies where survival heavily relied on collective efforts. The early roots of relationship anxiety can be traced back to this era, when primitive humans faced numerous uncertainties, including food scarcity, environmental threats, and the constant fear of predators. In such an unpredictable environment, individuals prioritized their personal safety over establishing and maintaining stable relationships. As a result, early humans exhibited a high degree of independence and a disinclination towards long-term commitments—a reflection of the anxieties ingrained within their survival instincts.

Ancient Civilizations: The Emergence of Patriarchy and Societal Expectations

With the rise of ancient civilizations like Mesopotamia, Egypt, and Greece, social relationships became more complex, and the seeds of relationship anxiety were sown. As early societies began forming into larger communities, the societal structures became increasingly patriarchal, with men assuming dominant roles and women being subjected to their authority. This shift in power dynamics created a breeding ground for relationship anxiety, as women, in particular, faced heightened vulnerability and anxieties regarding their safety, status, and overall well-being. Similarly, men experienced anxiety surrounding their societal expectations and the fear of potential challenges to their authority.

Feudal Societies: Love, Marriage, and the Social Contract

Throughout the feudal period in Europe, relationship anxiety further evolved due to the growing significance of love and marriage as a means of solidifying alliances, acquiring wealth, and perpetuating social hierarchies. As feudal societies became more stratified, noble families sought to secure marriages that offered economic, political, and social advantages. In this context, relationship anxiety transcended personal feelings and took on a broader societal dimension. The pressure to foster harmonious relationships, maintain familial honor, and fulfill the expectations of wider social circles induced profound anxiety in individuals, who were caught between personal desires and societal obligations.

Industrial Revolution: The Shift to Modern Romantic Relationships

The industrial revolution brought profound social and economic changes that revolutionized the nature of human relationships. As the agrarian system disintegrated and people migrated to cities in search of work, traditional social ties started to unravel, leaving individuals feeling disconnected and insecure. The emergence of a middle class and the rise of industrial capitalism also transformed the way romantic relationships were perceived. Love, previously seen as a consequence of marriage, began to be romanticized as the foundation of relationships—a shift that contributed to a new breed of relationship anxiety.

The advent of urbanization introduced new challenges: working long hours, geographical mobility, and increased exposure to diverse social circles. These factors disrupted traditional norms and exposed individuals to a myriad of romantic possibilities, consequently intensifying anxiety about making the right choice of partner, as well as fears of infidelity or abandonment. Furthermore, rapidly evolving societal values and gender dynamics placed additional pressure on individuals to conform to changing expectations, causing heightened anxiety about meeting cultural standards and maintaining relationship compatibility.

The Modern Era: Insecurity in a Hyperconnected World

As we progress into the modern era characterized by technological advancements and globalization, relationship anxiety continues to evolve. The digital age has brought both benefits and challenges, offering access to an unprecedented number of potential romantic partners while simultaneously creating an environment of heightened comparison, insecurity, and fear of missing out (FOMO). Social media platforms and online dating have increased relationship anxiety by amplifying societal pressures, promoting unrealistic standards of beauty, and facilitating constant comparison between one's own relationship and others.

Moreover, the rapid pace of modern life, combined with the constant connectivity, has further contributed to relationship anxiety. The ability to be constantly in touch with partners, albeit physically distant, has given rise to the fear of being "ghosted" or lack of immediate responses, triggering anxieties about the stability, commitment, and level of emotional investment within a relationship.

Reflecting on the historical perspectives of relationship anxiety allows us to better understand its complexities, roots, and multifaceted nature. From the primitive anxieties of survival to the intricate societal expectations of medieval feudal systems and the modern pressures of technological advancements, relationship anxiety has remained a persistent aspect of human experiences. Acknowledging and exploring these historical origins enables us to develop a more comprehensive understanding of relationship anxiety and, ultimately, work towards cultivating healthier, more fulfilling romantic connections in the future.

Modern Love's Challenge: How Today's World Exacerbates Heart's Turmoil

In this fast-paced and ever-evolving world, love has become a complex tapestry of emotions, desires, and challenges. The pursuit of love has always been a tumultuous journey, but in today's interconnected and technology-driven society, our hearts face an array of unique trials. From the impact of social media to the concept of instant gratification, this chapter explores how the modern world amplifies the already existing turmoil of the human heart.

The Illusion of Connection:

One of the greatest challenges of modern love lies in the illusion of connection perpetuated by social media. Platforms like Facebook, Instagram, and Twitter offer glimpses into the lives of others, creating a false sense of intimacy and constant comparison. The carefully curated feeds showcasing seemingly perfect relationships and happy moments can fuel insecurity and discontentment in our own lives. The constant exposure to others' relationships can lead to distress and dissatisfaction, resulting in a constant pursuit of unrealistic expectations, and ultimately exacerbating the turmoil in our hearts.

The Rise of Online Dating:

With the advent of online dating, the search for love has taken a digital turn. Swipe left, swipe right - it has become that simple to seek partners or potential love interests. However, this shift towards convenience comes with its own set of challenges. The abundance of choices presented in online dating can create a paradox of choice, causing anxiety and indecisiveness. This overload of options fosters a culture of disposable relationships, where it becomes easier to replace one partner with another, further deepening the heart's turmoil.

The Hookup Culture:

In the modern world, casual encounters have become more prevalent than ever before. The hookup culture lays a foundation for superficial interactions devoid of emotional depth. With carefully crafted online profiles, individuals can present themselves in a specific light, emphasizing their desirable traits while conveniently hiding their vulnerabilities. This transformation of dating into a purely physical and temporary affair not only exacerbates the turmoil in our hearts but also hinders the development of meaningful connections.

Instant Gratification and Relationship Expectations:

Today's society thrives on instant gratification - we want things, and we want them now. This mindset impacts our approach to relationships as well, where we expect immediate reciprocation of love and affection. The notion of working through hardships and investing time and effort in nurturing a relationship seems almost foreign. The lack of patience and unrealistic expectations can strain even the most promising love stories, leaving our hearts in a constant state of turmoil.

Fear of Missing Out (FOMO):

Fear of Missing Out (FOMO) has become an inherent part of our modern lives. We are bombarded with images and stories of others' seemingly perfect relationships, making us question the choices we've made. The constant fear of not living up to societal standards can lead to feelings of inadequacy and self-doubt, heightening the turmoil within our hearts. FOMO not only affects our peace of mind but also affects our ability to fully invest in our own relationships, as we are tempted to constantly seek validation elsewhere.

The Erosion of Privacy:

In the virtual realm of social media, one's private life is subject to public scrutiny. Intimate moments and relationship details are often shared with the world, diminishing the sacredness and vulnerability that love should entail. The erosion of privacy erodes trust and intimacy, further deepening the turmoil in our hearts. The constant exposure and potential for public shaming or judgment can hinder the development of genuine connections, leaving individuals guarded and emotionally closed off.

Navigating the terrain of love has always been a challenge, but the modern world seems to amplify the turmoil that exists within our hearts. From the illusion of connection created by social media to the pressures of instant gratification and the fear of missing out, our hearts face an array of unique obstacles.

However, by recognizing the impact of these challenges and striving for genuine connections in an increasingly impersonal world, we can triumph over the turmoil and find love that is meaningful, fulfilling, and lasting.

Shared Struggles: Prevalence and Impact on Personal Connections

Life often presents us with various challenges, shaping our experiences and molding our identity. These struggles, both personal and shared, influence how we perceive ourselves and connect with others. In this chapter, we delve into the prevalent nature of shared struggles and explore their impact on personal connections. Through our collective experiences, we perceive the importance of empathy, compassion, and understanding when navigating the complexities of human relationships.

Chapter One: Understanding Shared Struggles

1.1 Defining Shared Struggles:

Shared struggles can be understood as common challenges, difficulties, or obstacles faced by individuals or communities. These challenges could range from personal hardships like loss, illness, or self-doubt to societal issues such as discrimination, poverty, or political unrest. Shared struggles can be experienced individually or collectively, bringing people together through a shared sense of empathy and understanding.

1.2 Prevalence of Shared Struggles:

Shared struggles are an inherent part of the human condition, affecting people from all walks of life, regardless of age, gender, social background, or cultural differences. While the nature and severity of these struggles may vary, they bind us together by highlighting our shared vulnerabilities and universal experiences.

Chapter Two: The Impact of Shared Struggles on Personal Connections

2.1 Fostering Empathy and Understanding:

Shared struggles have a profound impact on personal connections by fostering empathy and understanding. When we encounter someone who has experienced a similar struggle, we are more likely to empathize, as we can relate to their feelings, emotions, and challenges. This shared empathy often forms the bedrock of deep, meaningful connections, nurturing a sense of belonging and support.

2.2 Breaking Down Barriers:

Shared struggles also have the potential to break down barriers and dissolve prejudices. When we encounter another person facing a similar challenge, we are forced to confront our assumptions and biases. The realization that someone unlike ourselves can face the same difficulties humanizes both parties, promoting inclusivity, and eroding societal divisions.

2.3 Building Support Networks:

Shared struggles bring individuals together, enabling the formation of support networks. When someone faces a challenge, having someone who understands can provide invaluable emotional support, guidance, and encouragement. These networks can create a sense of community, allowing individuals to lean on each other during times of adversity, bolstering their resilience and confidence.

Chapter Three: Navigating Shared Struggles in Relationships

3.1 Intentional Conversations:

Navigating shared struggles within personal connections often requires open and intentional communication. Sharing our experiences and challenges with trusted individuals creates a safe space for vulnerability and fosters trust. Through actively listening and validating each other's emotions, we can develop deeper connections and provide the necessary support.

3.2 Cultivating Empathy:

Empathy is a crucial attribute when offering support to those facing similar struggles. By putting ourselves in another's shoes, we enable a genuine understanding of their emotions, validating their experiences, and creating stronger bonds. Nurturing empathy involves actively seeking to understand, providing comfort, and offering assistance or resources if needed.

3.3 Recognizing Boundaries and Individual Experiences:

While shared struggles can create connections, it is vital to recognize that individuals respond and cope with challenges differently. Personal journeys can diverge, even in the face of similar struggles. It is important to respect each person's unique experience and avoid imposing our own expectations or narratives onto their narrative. Embracing differences nurtures inclusivity and strengthens personal connections.

Chapter Four: Lessons Learned from Shared Struggles

4.1 Personal Growth and Resilience:

Shared struggles provide opportunities for personal growth and resilience-building. By facing and overcoming challenges, we develop newfound strength, wisdom, and a deeper understanding of ourselves. These transformative experiences often shape our perception of the world and enhance our ability to relate to and support others.

4.2 The Power of Collective Action:

Shared struggles can galvanize communities and ignite movements for social change. By unifying in the face of adversity, people can amplify their voices, advocate for justice, and create lasting societal transformations. The collective power generated from shared struggles showcases the strength of human connections and the potential for positive change.

Shared struggles are an integral part of our human experience. By acknowledging and embracing these challenges, we pave the way for personal growth, deepen our connections, and foster empathy and compassion towards others. Navigating shared struggles within personal connections requires open communication, intentional empathy, and recognition of individual experiences. Ultimately, it is through shared struggles that we find strength, learn valuable lessons, and build the resilient human connections that enrich our lives.

Chapter 2: The Roots of Anxiety in Relationships

In the intricate web of human relationships, anxiety often lurks beneath the surface, exerting its influence on our interactions with others. Whether it be in romantic partnerships, friendships, or family dynamics, anxiety can seep into the very fabric of our connections, shaping how we relate, communicate, and form bonds. To truly understand and navigate these complexities, we must delve into the roots of anxiety in relationships. This chapter aims to explore these roots, shedding light on the underlying causes and offering insights to help individuals cultivate healthier, more fulfilling connections.

The Shaping of Attachment Styles

One of the primary contributors to relationship anxiety lies in the formation of attachment styles during childhood. Psychologist John Bowlby introduced the concept of attachment theory, explaining how early experiences with caregivers lay the groundwork for our adult relationships. When children experience consistent, nurturing care, they develop secure attachment styles, which enable them to form trusting, balanced relationships in adulthood.

However, when caregivers are inconsistent, neglectful, or overly intrusive, children may develop anxious or avoidant attachment styles. Those who develop anxious attachment styles tend to crave reassurance and fear abandonment, leading to persistent relationship anxiety. On the other hand, individuals with avoidant attachment styles may struggle with intimacy, often displaying emotional distance or difficulty in forming deep connections.

The Perils of Insecurity

Insecurity serves as another root of anxiety in relationships. One's sense of self-worth and confidence heavily influences their ability to engage in healthy connections. Individuals plagued by self-doubt or a negative self-image may constantly seek validation from their partners, leading to heightened anxiety when their legitimacy is questioned.

Moreover, past experiences of rejection or betrayal can embed deep-seated fears, making it challenging for individuals to trust others fully. These fears may manifest as excessive jealousy, possessiveness, or constant suspicion, ultimately causing strain in relationships.

Communication Breakdown

Effective communication serves as the lifeblood of any successful relationship. However, anxiety can profoundly impact one's ability to communicate openly and honestly. When consumed by anxiety, individuals may struggle to express their needs, concerns, or desires, fearing rejection or judgment.

Additionally, anxiety can distort how we interpret others' words and actions, leading to misunderstandings or unnecessary conflicts. The anxious mind tends to amplify perceived slights or dismissals, often viewing them through a lens of fear or insecurity. Consequently, open and authentic communication becomes compromised, as anxieties overpower rationality and empathy.

The Cycle of Interdependence

In many relationships, interdependence exists, forming the backbone of emotional connection. However, this very interdependence can also fuel relationship anxiety. Fear of overreliance or abandonment can drive individuals to adopt people-pleasing behaviors or exhibit excessive reassurance-seeking tendencies. These behaviors may temporarily alleviate anxiety but ultimately erode true authenticity and inhibit the growth of healthy, balanced partnerships. Furthermore, the cycle of anxious-dependent behavior can inadvertently reinforce relationship anxiety. As anxious individuals seek reassurance or cling to their partners, the other person may feel overwhelmed or trapped. This can lead to emotional distancing, as the partner feels suffocated or drained by the anxious dynamics. Thus, a self-perpetuating cycle of anxiety and insecurity forms, breeding further strain on the relationship.

The Role of Trauma

Traumatic experiences, whether stemming from childhood or later in life, can significantly impact one's ability to navigate relationships. When individuals have endured abuse, neglect, or other forms of trauma, the resulting anxiety and hypervigilance can linger, affecting their interactions with others.

For survivors of trauma, forming healthy, trusting relationships can be deeply challenging. Lingering fears, emotional flashbacks, or difficulty in setting boundaries may obstruct their journey towards intimacy. It is crucial for individuals carrying the weight of trauma to prioritize healing and seek support, allowing them to work through their anxieties and foster healthier relationships.

Chapter 2 has explored the roots of anxiety in relationships, shining light on the multifaceted factors that contribute to this pervasive issue. From the shaping of attachment styles in childhood to the impact of insecurity, communication breakdowns, the cycle of interdependence, and the role of trauma, we have uncovered the complexity of anxiety's influence on our connections with others. Understanding these roots allows individuals to cultivate self-awareness, recognizing how their own anxieties may impact their relationships. By acknowledging and addressing these anxieties, one can embark on a journey of personal growth, fostering healthier, more fulfilling connections based on trust, empathy, and effective communication.

Though this chapter has merely scratched the surface, it is our hope that the insights shared will propel readers towards further exploration and growth, empowering them to navigate the intricate dance of relationships with heightened understanding and resilience.

Childhood Shadows: How Early Attachments Influence Heart's Jitters

Childhood is a time of innocence, wonder, and discovery. It is during this phase of life that we form our earliest attachments and lay the foundation for our future relationships. The bonds we form with our caregivers play a crucial role in shaping our emotional well-being and influencing how we navigate the intricacies of love and intimacy in our adult lives. In this chapter, we delve into the fascinating world of childhood attachments and explore how they can impact the "heart's jitters" as we grow older.

Understanding Attachment Theory

To comprehend the profound influence of childhood attachments on our emotional lives, we must turn to the groundbreaking work of British psychiatrist John Bowlby and his attachment theory. Bowlby proposed that infants are biologically predisposed to seek proximity and emotional connection with their primary caregivers, typically their mothers. These early attachments are crucial for survival, as they provide security, warmth, and nourishment.

Bowlby classified attachment styles into four main categories: secure, anxious-ambivalent, anxious-avoidant, and disorganized. A secure attachment is typically characterized by a healthy balance of independence and dependence, with the child feeling safe to explore the world while knowing their caregiver is available to provide support when needed. Anxious-ambivalent attachment is marked by excessive clinginess and fear of abandonment, while anxious-avoidant attachment involves a child developing a dismissive attitude towards their caregiver, often due to inconsistent responsiveness. Disorganized attachment stems from significant trauma or neglect and can manifest as confusion and fear in relationships.

Impacts of Childhood Attachments

The attachment style we develop in childhood sets the stage for how we relate to others later in life. A secure attachment lays the groundwork for healthy, fulfilling relationships built on trust, emotional availability, and effective communication. These individuals tend to exhibit less anxiety and insecurity in their romantic partnerships and possess a greater capacity for intimacy.

Conversely, those who experienced anxious-ambivalent attachments may struggle with excessive neediness, jealousy, and a constant fear of rejection in their adult relationships. They may constantly seek reassurance and struggle with a fear of abandonment, which can put a strain on their romantic connections.

Individuals with an anxious-avoidant attachment style, on the other hand, often develop a strong fear of intimacy due to experiences of emotional unavailability or neglect in their early years. They may exhibit avoidant behaviors, such as an aversion to commitment or emotional closeness, in an attempt to protect themselves from potential hurt. These individuals often find it challenging to trust others, leading to difficulties in forming lasting and meaningful relationships.

The impact of disorganized attachment is perhaps the most profound and complex. Children who experience trauma, abuse, or neglect may develop an insecure and disorganized attachment style, resulting in a range of emotional and behavioral challenges in later life. They may struggle with regulating emotions, experience intense fear or anger, and find it difficult to establish stable and nurturing relationships.

Breaking Free from Childhood Shadows

Though our childhood experiences lay the groundwork for our attachment styles, it is essential to remember that they do not dictate our destinies. With self-awareness, introspection, and the willingness to heal, it is possible to overcome the shadows of our past and develop healthier relationship patterns.

Therapy, particularly attachment-based therapies like Integrated

Developmental Therapy (IDT), can provide a safe and supportive environment for individuals to explore their early attachments and work through any unresolved trauma. By examining the patterns established in childhood, individuals can learn to identify triggers and develop healthier coping mechanisms, leading to improved emotional well-being and more fulfilling relationships.

Developing self-compassion is another crucial aspect of breaking free from childhood shadows. Understanding that our experiences were not our fault and extending kindness and forgiveness to ourselves can facilitate the healing process. Engaging in self-care practices, such as mindfulness, journaling, and cultivating healthy boundaries, can aid in developing a healthier sense of self and fostering a deeper understanding of our emotional needs.

Childhood shadows cast a long-lasting impact on our emotional lives. The attachments we form in our formative years can influence our capacity for love, trust, and intimacy well into adulthood. Recognizing the influence of early attachments and seeking support to heal from any traumatic experiences can pave the way for healthier and more fulfilling relationships. By shedding light on these childhood shadows, we can embark on a journey of self-discovery, ultimately leading to greater emotional well-being, resilience, and a heart free from jitters.

Genetic Ties: The Biological Basis of Relationship Anxiety

Relationships are the cornerstone of the human experience, shaping our lives and providing us with emotional support, companionship, and love. However, for some individuals, the mere thought of entering into a romantic relationship can trigger significant anxiety and distress. This phenomenon, commonly known as relationship anxiety, affects millions of people worldwide and can have a detrimental impact on their mental and emotional well-being.

In recent years, researchers have started to explore the genetic underpinnings of relationship anxiety, seeking to uncover the biological factors that contribute to this complex and often debilitating condition. This chapter aims to delve into the world of genetic ties and shed light on the biological basis of relationship anxiety.

The Role of Genetics:

Genetics play a crucial role in shaping our mental and emotional landscape. While the field of genetic research is still in its early stages, numerous studies have indicated that our DNA can influence various aspects of our personality, temperament, and emotional well-being. By examining the genetic component of relationship anxiety, scientists hope to gain a deeper understanding of its origins and potentially develop more effective treatments.

Heritability of Relationship Anxiety:

Research suggests that relationship anxiety has a heritable component. Twin and family studies have shown that individuals with a family history of anxiety disorders, including relationship anxiety, are more likely to develop the condition themselves. These findings point to the presence of specific genetic variations that may increase vulnerability to relationship-related fears and insecurities.

Candidate Genes:

Scientists have identified several candidate genes that might be associated with relationship anxiety. One such gene is the serotonin transporter gene, which plays a crucial role in regulating serotonin levels – a neurotransmitter linked to mood and anxiety disorders. Variants of this gene have been found to contribute to the development of anxiety-related conditions, including social anxiety and phobias, suggesting a potential connection to relationship anxiety as well.

Another gene of interest is the oxytocin receptor gene. Oxytocin is often referred to as the "love hormone" due to its involvement in social bonding and attachment behaviors. Variations in the oxytocin receptor gene may affect the individual's ability to form and maintain close relationships, leading to heightened feelings of anxiety and insecurity.

Epigenetics and Relationship Anxiety:

In addition to the influence of genetic variations, recent studies have highlighted the role of epigenetics in the development of relationship anxiety. Epigenetics refers to modifications in gene expression that do not involve changes in the DNA sequence itself but can be influenced by environmental factors and experiences.

Researchers have found that early childhood experiences, such as parental bonding and childhood trauma, can trigger epigenetic changes that affect emotional regulation and stress responses. These alterations may, in turn, increase the risk of developing relationship anxiety later in life. Understanding the complex interplay between genetics and environmental factors is crucial in comprehending the biological basis of relationship anxiety fully.

Neurotransmitters and the Brain:

When exploring the biological basis of relationship anxiety, it is essential to examine the brain's role and the neurotransmitters involved. The amygdala, a part of the brain responsible for processing emotions and fear responses, has been implicated in anxiety disorders. Studies suggest that increased amygdala activation and reduced prefrontal cortex activity may contribute to heightened anxiety levels.

Neurotransmitters such as serotonin, dopamine, and norepinephrine also play a significant role in defining our emotional responses. Imbalances in these neurotransmitters have been associated with various anxiety disorders, including relationship anxiety. Understanding how these neurotransmitters interact with genetic factors is critical to unraveling the complexities of relationship anxiety.

Future Directions and Implications:

While our understanding of the genetic basis of relationship anxiety is still evolving, these discoveries have important implications for the future of mental health treatment. Armed with knowledge about the genetic and biological underpinnings of relationship anxiety, clinicians may be able to develop more targeted and personalized therapeutic interventions.

By tailoring treatment approaches to individual genetic profiles, it may be possible to enhance the effectiveness of therapy and reduce the burden of this pervasive condition. Moreover, further research into the genetic basis of relationship anxiety may help destigmatize the condition and promote a greater understanding and empathy for those affected.

Relationship anxiety is a complex and multifaceted condition that can significantly impact an individual's ability to form and maintain healthy relationships. By examining the genetic ties and understanding the biological basis of this anxiety, we can gain valuable insights into its etiology and potentially develop more effective treatments.

As scientists continue to unravel the intricate connections between genetics, the brain, and relationship anxiety, it is crucial to approach this research with empathy and a holistic understanding. By embracing a comprehensive perspective that encompasses both the biological and psychosocial aspects of relationship anxiety, we can work towards a future where individuals struggling with this condition find solace and support.

Past Loves, Present Fears: How Previous Relationships Affect Current Anxiety

Love relationships hold a significant place in our lives, shaping our emotional well-being, and influencing our overall mental health. While romantic relationships can bring immense joy and fulfillment, they can also leave lasting imprints that may manifest as anxiety in future relationships. In this chapter, we will explore the intricate connection between past loves and present fears, delving into how previous relationships can impact our current anxiety levels and understanding the mechanisms behind these effects.

The Marks of Past Loves:

Just as time leaves its mark on our physical selves, love and relationships leave their imprint on our emotional landscapes. Previous relationships can shape our perceptions, expectations, and beliefs about love, creating a foundation on which future relationships are built. These imprints become ingrained in our minds and can generate anxiety when similar patterns or situations arise in subsequent relationships.

Attachment Styles and Their Influence:

Psychologists have identified various attachment styles, which develop based on our earliest experiences with caregivers and significant others. These attachment styles provide a framework to understand how our past relationships can influence our present experiences. Those with anxious or anxious-avoidant attachment styles often exhibit higher levels of relationship anxiety. The fear of rejection or abandonment stemming from previous relationships can lead to a heightened sense of hypervigilance and anxiety in new relationships.

Unresolved Emotional Baggage:

Unresolved emotional baggage from past relationships can haunt us, even after the relationship has ended. Experiences such as betrayal, infidelity, or emotional abuse leave deep wounds that can impact our trust, vulnerability, and overall sense of security. As we enter new relationships, this unresolved emotional baggage can trigger anxiety, causing us to fear repeating past patterns and leading to a constant state of fear and apprehension.

Comparison and Self-Doubt:

Past relationships can also influence our self-perception and self-worth, which in turn affects our current anxiety levels. If we have experienced rejection, criticism, or comparison in previous relationships, we may develop a fear of not being enough or a constant doubt about our relationship's stability. The never-ending comparison with past partners can create a strong fear of not measuring up, leading to anxiety and an inability to fully trust in our current relationships.

Trauma and Post-Traumatic Relationship Anxiety:

In some cases, past relationships can leave individuals with traumatic experiences that shape their future love lives. Emotional, physical, or sexual abuse can have a profound impact on mental health, creating post-traumatic relationship anxiety. Individuals with this type of anxiety may struggle with trust, intimacy, and developing healthy emotional connections due to the fear of re-experiencing past trauma. Healing from such trauma often requires therapy and support to cultivate a sense of safety in future relationships.

The Role of Memory and Cognitive Bias:

Memory and cognitive biases play a crucial role in the way past relationships affect our current anxiety levels. Our minds tend to remember negative experiences more vividly than positive ones, leading to an overgeneralization of past pain in our current relationships. Cognitive biases, such as hindsight bias or confirmation bias, can distort our perceptions, reinforcing anxiety-provoking beliefs and expectations. Being aware of these biases can help individuals to challenge and reshape their thoughts, reducing anxiety and allowing for healthier relationship experiences.

Breaking Cycles and Building Resilience:

While the impact of past relationships on present anxiety may seem overwhelming, it is essential to remember that we have the power to break these cycles and build resilience. Recognizing the patterns and triggers that contribute to anxiety is the first step towards healing. Seeking therapy or counseling can provide individuals with a safe space to explore their past, process unresolved emotions, and develop coping mechanisms to manage anxiety in current relationships. Building self-love, practicing self-compassion, and prioritizing personal growth are also vital components of breaking free from the anxiety caused by past loves.

As we have explored in this chapter, past loves can leave a lasting impact on our present fears and anxieties. The wounds, traumas, and emotional imprints from previous relationships shape our perceptions, attachment styles, and self-perception. However, by acknowledging and addressing these past experiences, we can overcome anxiety and cultivate healthier relationships. Understanding the mechanisms through which our past influences our present is a crucial step towards building resilience, fostering trust, and embracing love with open hearts and minds.

Societal Pressures: The Impact of Cultural Expectations on the Heart's Balance

In today's fast-paced and interconnected world, it's impossible to overlook the enormous influence that societal pressures have on individuals. While societal norms and cultural expectations can shape and guide our behavior to an extent, they can also create a significant burden on our emotional well-being. This chapter explores the intricate relationship between societal pressures and the delicate balance of one's heart—both metaphorically and literally, looking at the consequences such pressures can have on individuals. We delve into how cultural expectations can impact mental health, relationships, and physical well-being, shedding light on this complex phenomenon.

Section 1: The Impact of Performance-based Culture

One of the most prevailing societal pressures is the relentless pursuit of success and the fear of failure. In performance-based cultures, individuals are frequently measured by their achievements, leading to immense pressure and anxiety. The constant need to meet or exceed societal expectations places an enormous strain on the heart, both figuratively and biologically. The emotional toll of this pressure can manifest in various forms, such as anxiety disorders, depression, or burnout. Additionally, the physiological implications of chronic stress can lead to cardiovascular issues, potentially disrupting the heart's balance.

Section 2: Cultural Expectations and the Search for Identity

Cultural expectations often dictate how individuals should think, behave, and present themselves to society. While these expectations can provide a sense of grounding and belonging, they can also stifle individuality and self-expression. The conflict between conforming to societal norms and the longing for personal authenticity creates an inner struggle within the heart. Suppressing one's true identity to meet cultural expectations can lead to feelings of emptiness, disconnection, and internal conflict. The heart's delicate equilibrium may be disrupted when authenticity is compromised, impacting emotional well-being and overall satisfaction in life.

Section 3: Relationships and the Burden of Societal Expectations

Societal pressures extend beyond the individual and seep into the realm of relationships. Cultural expectations dictate who we should love, how we should love, and under what circumstances love is deemed acceptable. These expectations can put tremendous strain on individuals and their relationships, leading to heartbreak, disappointment, and even heart disease. The burden of societal prejudices and judgments can hinder individuals from pursuing genuine connections and may contribute to feelings of isolation and loneliness. As the heart yearns for authentic connection, societal expectations can disrupt its delicate balance, negatively impacting emotional well-being.

Section 4: Body Image and the Quest for Perfection

In today's image-driven society, a deep-rooted cultural expectation revolves around physical appearance. The perpetual pursuit of the ideal body can have devastating effects on an individual's mental and physical well-being. Body dysmorphia, eating disorders, and body shaming are some of the consequences of societal pressures to conform to certain beauty standards. The heart's equilibrium is disrupted when self-worth becomes closely linked to one's physical appearance, leading to feelings of inadequacy and vulnerability. This imbalance not only affects mental health but can also lead to cardiovascular problems, as chronic stress takes its toll.

Section 5: Breaking Free from Societal Pressures

While societal pressures can have a profound impact on the heart's balance, it is essential to recognize that individuals have the power to break free from these constraints. Cultivating self-awareness, resilience, and authenticity can help individuals navigate the complexities of societal expectations without compromising their well-being. Embracing diversity, challenging norms, and fostering self-acceptance are paramount in restoring the heart's equilibrium. By reframing cultural expectations and focusing on organic personal growth, individuals can forge a path towards a more fulfilling life, unburdened by the weight of societal pressures.

Section 6: Embracing Cultural Dynamism

Finding a harmonious balance between societal pressures and personal well-being entails a reevaluation of cultural norms. As societies evolve and cultural dynamics shift, it becomes crucial to question the values and expectations that have shaped our lives. Rigid adherence to outdated or oppressive traditions can perpetuate societal pressures and hinder personal growth. Embracing cultural dynamism allows for the creation of a more inclusive and compassionate society, freeing individuals from the weight of unrealistic expectations and paving the way for a balanced heart. Societal pressures have an undeniable impact on the heart's delicate balance. From performance-based cultures to the suppression of personal authenticity, onto the burden of conforming relationships and body image expectations, these pressures can disrupt emotional well-being and physical health. However, by fostering self-awareness, embracing diversity, and challenging cultural norms, individuals can liberate themselves from the grip of societal expectations. It is through this freedom that the heart's equilibrium can be restored, enabling individuals to live authentically and harmoniously within themselves and with others.

Chapter 3: The Manifestation of Heart's Disturbance

The human heart is a fascinating entity. It is not merely a physical organ, pumping blood within our bodies, but a metaphorical reservoir of emotions, desires, and passions. Throughout history, countless artists, thinkers, and philosophers have endeavored to interpret and understand the complexity of this enigmatic organ. In the depths of the heart, beneath the surface of our conscious mind, lie the seeds of profound disturbances waiting to manifest themselves.

1. The Prelude to Descent

Within the dark recesses of the heart, the seeds of a disturbance take root, often unbeknownst to the individual harboring them. These seeds can germinate from a variety of experiences, including moments of great joy or profound sorrow. There exists within the human psyche an unyielding connection between happiness and turmoil, as if they feed off each other, nurturing the very essence of our being.

2. The Stirring of Unease

As the disturbance within the heart begins to grow, it takes on a life of its own, moving steadily closer to the threshold of consciousness. Like a slumbering beast, it stirs and unsettles the peace of mind. Simple inconveniences and daily frustrations are amplified, becoming magnified lenses through which the individual views the world.

In this state, every word uttered, every gesture made, is deconstructed and analyzed for hidden meaning. Trust evaporates, replaced by suspicion and doubt. The once harmonious symphony of life becomes discordant, the notes clashing brutally against each other.

3. The Unveiling of Inner Turmoil

When the disturbance reaches the surface, it manifests itself in myriad ways. Some individuals find solace in the catharsis of tears, allowing the pent-up emotions to flow freely. Others may exhibit fits of anger, displaced outrage seeking an outlet to express its overwhelming force. Yet, there are those who silently suffer, concealing their turmoil behind a mask of indifference or stoicism.

In these moments, clashes between reason and emotion become palpable. Rationality succumbs to the relentless assault of passion, leading to impulsive actions and irrational decisions. It is as if the heart takes control, usurping the reigns of governance from the mind, propelling the individual on an uncharted course.

4. The Wandering Path

Upon the manifestation of heart's disturbance, one embarks on a journey, uncertain of its destination or purpose. It is a path marred by confusion, self-doubt, and the agonizing battle between desires and obligations. Relationships are tested, loyalty questioned, and the foundation of one's existence shaken to the very core.

During this arduous trek, precious moments of clarity emerge from the chaos. Fleeting glimpses of self-reflection afford solace and provide space for contemplation. Through introspection, one may begin to discern the root cause of the disturbance, tracing its origins to buried memories or unresolved conflicts.

5. Reflections on the Manifestation

As the chapter on the manifestation of heart's disturbance draws to a close, a stark realization dawns upon the individual: the turmoil experienced is not merely a consequence of external circumstances but an integral part of their being. It is an intrinsic aspect of what makes us human—flawed, passionate, and endlessly in pursuit of understanding and fulfillment.

In recognizing this, the individual gains a newfound appreciation for the complexity and resilience of the human heart. It is not an organ to be feared or repressed but one to be embraced and understood. By acknowledging the manifestation of heart's disturbance, we tap into a wellspring of growth and self-discovery, unravelling the intricacies of our own emotional landscape.

While this text has explored the manifestation of heart's disturbance, it is important to remember that this phenomenon varies greatly from person to person. Some may experience turbulent emotions on a daily basis, while others may encounter this disturbance only sporadically throughout their lives.

The manifestation of heart's disturbance is an integral part of the human experience, serving as a catalyst for growth, introspection, and self-understanding. To truly comprehend the workings of our hearts, we must embrace the disturbances that emerge, for they illuminate the intricate tapestry of our existence.

Symptoms Speak: Recognizing Signs of Relationship Anxiety

Relationships are a fundamental aspect of human life. They provide us with love, companionship, and a sense of belonging. However, for some individuals, relationships can also be a source of anxiety and distress. Relationship anxiety is more common than we may think, and its symptoms can manifest in various ways. In this chapter, we will explore the signs of relationship anxiety and discuss strategies to recognize and manage this condition. By gaining a better understanding of these symptoms, we can build healthier and more fulfilling relationships.

Unveiling Relationship Anxiety:

Relationship anxiety can be defined as an excessive worry or fear surrounding intimate relationships. While it is normal to experience some level of anxiety in relationships, individuals with relationship anxiety often find it challenging to maintain healthy connections due to intense worry and insecurity. However, recognizing these symptoms is the first step towards managing and overcoming relationship anxiety.

1. Jealousy and Insecurity:

One of the most common symptoms of relationship anxiety is jealousy and insecurity. Individuals experiencing relationship anxiety may often feel threatened by their partner's interactions with others. They may become excessively possessive, check their partner's phone, or become overly suspicious without any concrete evidence. Jealousy can strain relationships and erode trust if left unaddressed.

2. Fear of Abandonment:

Fear of abandonment is another primary symptom of relationship anxiety. Individuals may constantly worry that their partner will leave them or withdraw their love and affection. This fear can be deeply rooted in past experiences or emotional attachment issues. The fear of abandonment often leads to clingy behaviors or an overwhelming need for constant reassurance from one's partner.

3. Overthinking and Catastrophizing:

Individuals with relationship anxiety tend to overthink and catastrophize scenarios relating to their relationship. They might obsessively analyze their partner's words and actions, searching for hidden meanings or potential signs of rejection. This perpetual rumination can lead to heightened anxiety and strained communication in the relationship.

4. Fear of Intimacy:

While relationships are built on emotional and physical intimacy, individuals with relationship anxiety may struggle with fear of intimacy. This fear often stems from a fear of vulnerability and the potential for emotional pain. Consequently, they may avoid closeness or become emotionally distant to protect themselves from anticipated hurt.

5. Perfectionism and Self-Doubt:

Relationship anxiety often overlaps with perfectionism and self-doubt. These individuals may place unrealistic expectations on themselves and their partners. They may believe that unless everything is perfect, their relationship will inevitably fail. This constant self-doubt can undermine self-esteem and perpetuate feelings of anxiety and dissatisfaction.

6. Difficulty in Trusting:

Trust is a crucial component of any healthy relationship. However, individuals with relationship anxiety often struggle to trust their partners fully. They may doubt their partner's intentions, question their loyalty, or feel unworthy of love. This lack of trust can cause strain and constant conflict within the relationship.

Recognizing and Acknowledging Relationship Anxiety:
Now that we have explored the various symptoms of relationship anxiety, it is essential to recognize and acknowledge these signs in oneself or in a loved one. Identifying relationship anxiety is crucial for seeking appropriate support and implementing effective strategies to manage this condition.

It is important to remember that relationship anxiety does not necessarily indicate that the relationship is inherently flawed or doomed to fail. Instead, it reflects an internal struggle within an individual that can be addressed through self-awareness and self-growth.

Strategies for Managing Relationship Anxiety:

Once relationship anxiety has been recognized, there are several strategies that individuals can employ to manage and overcome this condition. These strategies involve a combination of self-reflection, open communication with partners, and professional support when necessary.

1. Self-Awareness and Reflection:

Developing self-awareness is a fundamental step towards managing relationship anxiety. By identifying triggers, underlying fears, and patterns of anxious thinking, individuals can gain insights into their own insecurities and work towards managing them. Self-reflection exercises, such as journaling or therapy, can aid in this process.

2. Open Communication:

Open and honest communication with one's partner is essential in managing relationship anxiety. Sharing fears and concerns allows for mutual understanding and empathy. By openly discussing anxieties, expectations, and boundaries, couples can work together to create a safe and supportive environment where both partners feel heard and validated.

3. Establishing Boundaries:

Establishing clear boundaries is crucial in managing relationship anxiety. By setting healthy boundaries, individuals can alleviate some of the fears and uncertainties that drive relationship anxiety. These boundaries can include personal space, time for individual pursuits, and open discussions about acceptable behaviors within the relationship.

4. Seeking Professional Help:

In some instances, managing relationship anxiety may require the assistance of a mental health professional. Therapy can provide individuals with the tools and support necessary to navigate their anxieties effectively. Cognitive-behavioral therapy (CBT) and couples therapy have shown particular efficacy in addressing relationship anxiety.

Recognizing the signs of relationship anxiety is a vital step towards building healthier, more fulfilling relationships. By understanding the symptoms, individuals can work towards developing effective strategies to manage and overcome their anxieties. Whether through self-reflection, open communication, or seeking professional help, it is possible to cultivate relationships that are grounded in love, trust, and contentment. Remember, with the right support and self-care, relationship anxiety can be understood and managed, leading to happier and more satisfying connections.

The Cycle of Doubt: How Anxiety Reinforces Itself in the Heart

The heart, often described as a symbol of love and passion, is also a remarkable organ that serves as the center of our emotional experiences. It beats tirelessly, pumping life-giving blood to every part of our body. But just as it nourishes us, the heart can also be a breeding ground for doubt and anxiety, feeding into a relentless cycle that can be incredibly difficult to break free from.

In this chapter, we will delve into the intricate connections between anxiety and doubt, exploring the ways in which they reinforce one another within the depths of our hearts. By understanding the mechanisms that perpetuate this cycle, we can begin to dismantle it, allowing ourselves to find freedom and peace.

Anxiety, characterized by persistent worrying, restlessness, and a constant sense of unease, often finds its roots in doubt. Doubt, on the other hand, arises from uncertainty and a lack of confidence in oneself or the world around us. The two intertwine, creating a complex web that can overwhelm even the most resilient individuals.

Picture this: you wake up one morning, your heart racing for no apparent reason. Thoughts rush through your mind, questioning whether you possess the skills necessary to succeed in a new job. You doubt your ability to form meaningful connections with others and wonder if anyone truly cares about you. These doubts fuel your anxiety, further intensifying the physical sensations you experience.

The first step in understanding this cycle is to recognize that doubt often arises from our own negative self-talk. We begin to question our worth, abilities, and even our previous accomplishments. The more we doubt ourselves, the more anxious we become. This anxiety, in turn, reinforces our doubts, creating a never-ending loop of self-deprecation and fret.

Anxiety influences our perception of the world, distorting our view of ourselves, others, and the situations we encounter. Over time, we become trapped in a negative feedback loop, where our doubts fuel our anxiety, and our anxiety strengthens our doubts. It's as if we are constantly looking through a murky lens, unable to see beyond our own insecurities.

The cycle of doubt and anxiety doesn't only affect our thoughts and emotions; it takes a toll on our physical health as well. As anxiety tightens its grip, individuals often experience a plethora of symptoms such as headaches, muscle tension, sleep disturbances, and gastrointestinal issues. These physical manifestations of anxiety, in turn, reinforce the doubt. We question whether these symptoms are merely due to anxiety or if there is something more sinister lurking beneath the surface.

To break free from the cycle, we must take a step back and examine each element individually. Recognizing self-doubt as a result of negative self-talk is crucial. We must challenge our negative thoughts and replace them with self-compassion and positive affirmations. By consciously shifting our mindset, we can weaken the hold that doubt has on our hearts.

Similarly, managing anxiety involves acknowledging its presence and finding healthy coping mechanisms. Mindfulness practices, such as deep breathing and meditation, can help ground us in the present moment, alleviating anxiety's grip. Engaging in regular exercise, maintaining a balanced diet, and seeking therapy are additional avenues that can dismantle the cycle.

While challenging these negative patterns of thinking and incorporating these coping strategies is important, it is equally vital to examine the origins of our doubts. Often, self-doubt stems from past experiences, societal pressures, or unrealistic expectations. By reflecting on these underlying causes, we can gain a deeper understanding of ourselves and begin to reshape our beliefs.

Ultimately, breaking the cycle of doubt and anxiety requires patience and perseverance. It is a journey that necessitates self-reflection, self-compassion, and a willingness to challenge deeply ingrained patterns. But with time and effort, we can find solace in the knowledge that we are not defined by our doubts or our anxiety. We have the power to break free and cultivate a heart filled with love, confidence, and resilience.

Effects Beyond the Heart: Physical and Mental Impacts of Relationship Anxiety

Relationships are undoubtedly one of the most fulfilling aspects of life, providing us with love, support, and companionship. However, for many individuals, the journey of love can be accompanied by relationship anxiety. It is a state characterized by constant uncertainty, fear, and worry about the future of one's romantic partnership. While relationship anxiety primarily affects the heart, its impacts reverberate far beyond our emotional realm. In this chapter, we will delve into the physical and mental repercussions of relationship anxiety, shedding light on the multifaceted nature of this complex issue.

Physical Manifestations of Relationship Anxiety:

1. Insomnia and Sleep Disorders:
The turmoil of relationship anxiety can often invade our sleep, leading to insomnia and other sleep disturbances. Constantly worrying about the relationship's stability, future, or trust can cause difficulty in falling asleep or staying asleep throughout the night. Consequently, deprivation of quality sleep heightens fatigue, affects

cognitive abilities, and leaves individuals susceptible to a host of physical ailments.

2. Gastrointestinal Disturbances:

The gut-brain connection is evident when it comes to relationship anxiety. Persistent worry can trigger various gastrointestinal issues such as stomachaches, indigestion, diarrhea, and even irritable bowel syndrome (IBS). These digestive problems arise due to the intricate interaction between our emotions and the functioning of the digestive system, ultimately affecting our overall well-being.

3. Weakened Immune System:

Relationship anxiety can exert a significant toll on our immune system, leaving us more susceptible to illnesses. Chronic stress associated with relationship anxiety can disrupt immune functions, leading to increased vulnerability to colds, infections, and other ailments. The weakened immune response is a direct consequence of the body being constantly on high alert due to anxiety and stress.

4. Weight Fluctuations:

Few individuals may experience weight fluctuations as they navigate through relationship anxiety. Stress-related eating patterns, such as overeating or undereating, can disrupt our body's balance and lead to weight gain or loss. These changes may not only impact physical health but also dampen one's self-esteem and aggravate mental distress further.

Mental Ramifications of Relationship Anxiety:

1. Anxiety Disorders:

Experiencing relationship anxiety for an extended period can escalate to generalized anxiety disorder (GAD) or other anxiety-related conditions. GAD is characterized by excessive, chronic worrying that extends beyond relationship concerns and permeates other areas of life. This debilitating condition can hinder individuals' ability to function optimally, undermining their overall quality of life.

2. Depression and Mood Disorders:

The constant strain of relationship anxiety can progressively chip away at an individual's emotional well-being, often leading to depression or other mood disorders. Feelings of worthlessness, hopelessness, and despair may accompany relationship anxiety, leaving individuals feeling emotionally drained and overwhelmed by the weight of their worries.

3. Low Self-Esteem:

Relationship anxiety can gradually erode an individual's self-esteem, leading to feelings of self-doubt, unworthiness, and an unhealthy reliance on external validation. The constant fear of not being good enough or deserving of love can significantly impact one's self-perception, hindering personal growth, and fostering detrimental beliefs about oneself.

4. Impaired Decision-Making:

Relationship anxiety can impair an individual's ability to make sound decisions, both within and outside of their romantic relationship. The constant doubt and second-guessing can inhibit cognitive processes, making it challenging to evaluate situations objectively and make rational choices. This, in turn, can strain relationships further and hinder personal progress.

The intricacies of relationship anxiety extend far beyond matters of the heart. This chapter has explored the vast array of physical and mental repercussions that can arise from such anxiety, highlighting the significant toll it takes on individuals' overall well-being. The goal of this discussion is not to instill fear but to shed light on the multifaceted nature of relationship anxiety, providing insight and understanding that can potentially support those grappling with these challenges.

By recognizing the potential physical and mental impacts of relationship anxiety, we can begin to develop strategies to address and alleviate the distress it causes. It is imperative to seek support, both professional and personal, to navigate through relationship anxiety and restore balance to our lives. Remember, no one should face relationship anxiety alone, and with the right resources and support, we can regain control, heal, and form healthier, more fulfilling connections.

Ripples in the Pond: How Relationship Anxiety Affects Partners

Relationships are complex and multifaceted, often giving rise to a range of emotions and challenges. While some individuals thrive in the warmth of connection, others may find themselves caught in the tumultuous web of relationship anxiety. This chapter delves into the intricate nature of relationship anxiety and explores the profound impact it can have on the partners involved. By shedding light on this often misunderstood phenomenon, we hope to foster empathy, understanding, and help partners navigate the choppy waters together.

Understanding Relationship Anxiety:

Relationship anxiety, at its core, is the fear and uncertainty one experiences in their romantic partnership. It can manifest in various ways, such as incessant doubts about the relationship's longevity, fear of rejection or abandonment, or an overwhelming need for constant reassurance. These thoughts and emotions tend to create a sense of unease and can erode the foundation of a relationship over time.

The Source of Relationship Anxiety:

While relationship anxiety can be triggered by external factors, such as past traumas or infidelity, it often originates from internal insecurities. Deep-rooted fears of not being lovable or worthy of companionship can infiltrate one's thoughts and emotions, leading to a perpetual cycle of anxiety. Moreover, societal pressures and unrealistic expectations can exacerbate these anxieties, leaving individuals feeling trapped in a cycle of self-doubt.

The Impact on the Anxious Partner:

An individual grappling with relationship anxiety may find their thoughts consumed by worst-case scenarios. Constantly haunted by the fear of loss or rejection, they may excessively seek reassurance from their partner, leading to feelings of suffocation and frustration. This consistent need for validation can push their partner to the brink, unable to meet the escalating demands for reassurance and triggering a cascade of emotional turmoil.

The Impact on the Non-Anxious Partner:

While it is the anxious partner who primarily grapples with relationship anxiety, the non-anxious partner often bears the brunt of its consequences. Over time, the emotional labor of constantly soothing their partner's fears can become draining and overwhelming. It may lead to feelings of inadequacy, frustration, or even resentment, as the non-anxious partner struggles to understand and address their own needs within the relationship.

Communication and Relationship Anxiety:

Effective communication is paramount in mitigating the adverse effects of relationship anxiety. Anxious partners must learn to openly share their fears and concerns while non-anxious partners need to express their emotions and set healthy boundaries. By fostering an environment that encourages honest and compassionate dialogue, both partners can gain a clearer understanding of each other's needs, expectations, and anxieties. This can help diminish the ripple effect caused by relationship anxiety.

Challenging the Anxious Thought Patterns:

Cognitive-behavioral therapy (CBT) has shown great promise in helping individuals overcome relationship anxiety. By challenging and reframing negative thought patterns, CBT equips anxious partners with the tools necessary to identify and replace irrational beliefs with more realistic and positive ones. Through this process, they can break free from the grip of relationship anxiety and foster a healthier, more secure bond with their partner.

Support and Empathy as Allies:

Partnership in the face of relationship anxiety requires both empathy and support. The non-anxious partner can play a crucial role in creating a safe space by actively validating the anxious partner's emotions. Demonstrating patience, understanding, and actively working together to confront and address anxieties can pave the way toward healing and growth. Additionally, seeking professional help, such as couples therapy, can provide further guidance in navigating the complexities of relationship anxiety.

Embracing Self-Care:

Caring for oneself is vital for both partners involved in combating relationship anxiety. Engaging in self-care practices such as exercise, mindfulness, and individual therapy can alleviate stress and promote a sense of well-being. Encouraging each other to prioritize self-care not only strengthens the individual but also bolsters the relationship, enhancing resilience in the face of anxiety.

Relationship anxiety can cast a long, dark shadow on the path to a fulfilling, loving partnership. However, with understanding, open communication, professional guidance, and empathy, partners can break free from the grip of relationship anxiety. By collectively striving to create a secure, nurturing environment, couples can transform the ripples caused by relationship anxiety into waves of growth, connection, and love.

Chapter 4: The Heart's Guide to Understanding Partners with Anxiety

Anxiety is a common mental health condition that affects millions of people worldwide. The burdensome weight it places on individuals can be challenging to bear, but it also has significant implications for their relationships, particularly with their partners. This chapter aims to provide a heartfelt guide to help you navigate the complexities of having a partner with anxiety.

Understanding Anxiety:

To fully comprehend how anxiety impacts a partnership, it is crucial to grasp what anxiety truly is. Anxiety is more than just feeling nervous or stressed; it is an overwhelming sense of fear or worry that persists even in non-threatening situations. This constant presence of anxiety can greatly affect the emotional and mental well-being of those who experience it.

It is crucial to remember that anxiety is not a weakness or a flaw but a genuine mental health condition. Just like any other illness, it requires understanding, empathy, and support from both partners to ensure the creation of a safe and nurturing environment.

Recognizing Anxiety in Your Partner:

Anxiety manifests differently in each individual, but there are common signs to be mindful of. These may include excessive worrying, restlessness, irritability, difficulty concentrating, and physical symptoms such as increased heart rate and shallow breathing. By being observant and acknowledging these signs, you can better understand your partner's thoughts and emotions.

The Communication Dilemma:

Effective communication is the cornerstone of any healthy relationship. However, when one partner has anxiety, communication can become even more challenging. Anxiety tends to distort thoughts and trigger irrational fears, making it challenging for individuals to express their feelings openly and effectively.

As the supportive partner, it is essential to create a safe space for open dialogue. Encourage your partner to express their thoughts and emotions, actively listen without judgment, and validate their experiences. Assure them that their concerns are worthy of attention and that you are there to support them unconditionally.

Educate Yourself:

Knowledge is power, and educating yourself about anxiety will undoubtedly strengthen your relationship. Take the time to learn about the different types of anxiety disorders, their symptoms, and the available treatment options. Understanding the nuances of anxiety will enable you to provide the necessary support and reassurance that your partner needs.

Remember, however, that you are not expected to become an expert overnight. It is a continuous learning process, and your partner will appreciate your genuine efforts to understand their struggles.

Building Trust and Security:

Building trust and fostering a sense of security within a relationship is of paramount importance when one partner has anxiety. Anxiety often breeds insecurities and a constant fear of abandonment. Therefore, it is vital to reassure your partner regularly of your love, commitment, and loyalty.

Maintaining consistent open communication, setting healthy boundaries, and demonstrating your reliability will help alleviate some of your partner's anxieties. By creating a foundation built on trust and safety, you both can navigate the challenges ahead with greater resilience.

Supporting Healthy Coping Mechanisms:

Helping your partner develop and maintain healthy coping mechanisms is crucial for managing their anxiety. Encourage them to engage in activities that promote relaxation, such as exercise, meditation, or pursuing hobbies they enjoy. Together, explore mindfulness practices or seek professional guidance to develop coping skills that work specifically for them.

Remember that everyone's journey is unique, and what may work for one person may not work for another. Be patient and understanding as your partner discovers their preferred methods of managing anxiety.

The Power of Patience:

Living with anxiety means navigating a rollercoaster of emotions, insecurities, and uncertainty. It is essential to cultivate patience, as setbacks and relapses may occur along the way. Anxiety is not something that can be easily overcome, so avoid pressuring your partner with unrealistic expectations.

Offer your unwavering support during the difficult periods, reminding them that you are there for them without judgment or condition. Patience will help you both weather the storms together and emerge stronger as a couple.

Seeking Professional Help:

While your love and support play a crucial role in assisting your partner with anxiety, it is important to recognize the limitations of your help. Sometimes, seeking professional intervention is necessary. Encourage your partner to explore therapy options, such as cognitive-behavioral therapy (CBT) or medication if recommended by a mental health professional.

Remember that therapy is not a reflection of your inability to support your partner but a joint effort to ensure their well-being. Be supportive throughout the process, attending sessions together if appropriate, and celebrating the progress made along the way.

Understanding and supporting a partner with anxiety can be a challenging journey, but it is one that can strengthen your relationship in profound ways. By developing a compassionate understanding of anxiety, practicing effective communication, and offering unwavering support, you can create a nurturing environment that empowers your partner to manage their anxiety and grow together as a couple. Remember that each person's journey is unique, and patience, empathy, and continuous effort will be the building blocks that lead to a deeper, more resilient bond.

Listening to Silent Fears: Embracing a Partner's Relationship Anxiety

Love is a beautiful journey filled with joy, connection, and deep understanding. However, along this path, it is not uncommon for anxiety to creep into the hearts of both partners, silently poisoning the love they share. Relationship anxiety can manifest in various ways, causing insecurities, doubt, and fear of abandonment. In this chapter, we delve deep into understanding the complexities of relationship anxiety and explore ways to listen, support, and embrace a partner experiencing these silent fears.

Understanding Relationship Anxiety

Relationship anxiety is a pervasive feeling of unease and worry about the stability and future of a romantic relationship. It often stems from past experiences of trauma or failed relationships, leading individuals to question their own worthiness of love and their partner's commitment. These anxieties can be triggered by events or circumstances that activate deep-seated fears and insecurities.

Listening with Empathy

When confronted with a partner experiencing relationship anxiety, it is crucial to approach the situation with empathy and understanding. By actively listening, we give our partners the space to express their fears and concerns without judgment. Listening with empathy means setting aside our own preconceived notions and truly being present for our loved one.

1. Create a safe space: Provide a safe environment for open and honest communication. Assure your partner that their fears and concerns are valid and will be heard without judgment.

2. Active listening: Put aside distractions and actively engage in the conversation. Maintain eye contact, provide verbal and nonverbal cues to show that you are fully attentive to what they have to say.

3. Reflective responses: Summarize and clarify your partner's thoughts and emotions to show that you genuinely understand their perspective. This not only conveys empathy but also ensures that there is no misunderstanding.

4. Validation: Validate your partner's feelings and emotions by reiterating that their concerns are real and important. Avoid minimizing their anxieties or dismissing them as irrational.

Encouraging Open Dialogue

Building trust and fostering open dialogue is essential when addressing relationship anxiety. Encourage your partner to express their fears and concerns in a healthy manner, promoting a safe space and nurturing a deeper connection.

1. Regular check-ins: Cultivate a habit of regularly checking in with your partner about their emotional well-being and the state of your relationship. This allows for open discussions and early intervention before anxieties escalate.

2. Ask open-ended questions: Prompt your partner to share their thoughts and feelings by asking open-ended questions. This encourages a more detailed response and discourages simple yes/no answers, facilitating a deeper understanding of their anxieties.

3. Practice non-judgment: Demonstrate your commitment to understanding your partner by avoiding judgment and criticism. Remind them that their feelings are valid, and their anxieties should not be dismissed.

4. Be patient and compassionate: Relationship anxiety can be a long and winding road for both partners. Remember to be patient, allowing your loved one the time and space to work through their fears while providing unwavering support and compassion along the

way.

Providing Reassurance and Security

When gripped by relationship anxiety, individuals may seek reassurance and validation from their partners. Providing a sense of security can help ease their fears and strengthen the bond in your relationship.

1. Unconditional love: Communicate your love and commitment unconditionally. Reassure your partner that you will stand by them and support them through their anxieties, emphasizing that you are in this relationship for the long haul.

2. Express appreciation: Regularly express gratitude and appreciation for your partner's presence in your life. This reminds them of their value and reinforces their sense of importance within the relationship.

3. Establish clear boundaries: Establishing clear boundaries and providing consistency can be comforting for individuals experiencing relationship anxiety. This includes setting expectations and creating a safe framework within which both partners can express themselves.

4. Share experiences: Openly discuss your own vulnerabilities and

fears, as this can help normalize their anxieties and create a safe space for sharing. By sharing experiences, you encourage a sense of unity and understanding.

Love, with all its beauty and wonder, is not immune to anxiety. Embracing a partner's relationship anxiety requires patience, understanding, and active listening. By creating a safe space, encouraging open dialogue, and providing reassurance, we can strengthen the bond between partners, allowing love to triumph over fear.

Together, let us embark on a journey of understanding and compassion, supporting our loved ones as they navigate the depths of their silent fears.

Decoding Heart's Desires: Misunderstandings and Miscommunications in Anxious Relationships

In the intricate tapestry of human relationships, communication plays a pivotal role in shaping our experiences, particularly in romantic partnerships. However, misinterpretations and misunderstandings can often cloud the path toward true understanding, leading to anxiety and turmoil within the relationship. In this chapter, we will delve into the complexities of decoding heart's desires in anxious relationships, exploring the various aspects that contribute to miscommunications and shed light on the ways to navigate them.

1. The Anxious Attachment Style:

To truly grasp the dynamics of anxious relationships, it is crucial to understand the anxious attachment style. Individuals with an anxious attachment style tend to crave intimacy and fear abandonment, leading to heightened sensitivity and emotional reactivity within the relationship. Such anxieties can inadvertently affect communication, resulting in misaligned perceptions of desires and intentions.

2. The Role of Emotional Triggers:

Emotional triggers play a significant role in anxious relationships. These triggers stem from past experiences or insecurities and can ignite intense emotional responses. In these instances, communication often becomes distorted, with partners struggling to understand each other's needs and intentions. Unaddressed emotional triggers can further exacerbate miscommunications, breeding a cycle of anxiety within the relationship.

3. The Power of Nonverbal Communication:

Communication encompasses far more than just words; nonverbal cues can hold substantial meaning within a relationship. However, in anxious relationships, partners tend to misinterpret nonverbal signals, leading to misunderstandings and intensified anxiety. Deciphering nonverbal cues accurately involves recognizing and validating each other's emotions rather than making assumptions, fostering a more profound understanding of desires and intentions.

4. The Perils of Assumptions:

Assumptions often serve as silent culprits behind miscommunications in anxious relationships. Anxious individuals, driven by their fears and insecurities, may often jump to conclusions about their partner's intentions without seeking clarification. Such assumptions can create a distorted reality, fueling anxiety and mistrust. Overcoming this hurdle requires open and honest dialogue, where partners can express their concerns and clarify their intentions without judgment.

5. The Need for Active Listening:

Active listening forms the foundation for effective communication. Unfortunately, anxiety often hinders one's ability to listen attentively, as the mind becomes preoccupied with worries and insecurities. In anxious relationships, partners may misinterpret each other's words, leading to further misunderstandings and miscommunications. Engaging in active listening techniques, such as paraphrasing and validating each other's feelings, can bridge this gap and foster clearer communication channels.

6. The Role of Empathy:

Empathy is the key to unraveling the desires of the heart in anxious relationships. When one partner experiences heightened anxiety, the other's ability to empathize becomes crucial. Understanding and validating one's emotions can create a safe space for open and honest communication. Empathy helps in unraveling hidden desires, ensuring both partners feel heard, understood, and supported.

7. The Importance of Boundaries:

Boundaries are essential in every relationship, particularly in anxious ones. Anxiety can lead to blurred boundaries, as partners may overstep personal limits in their quest to seek reassurance and validate their fears. Forging healthy boundaries allows partners to respect each other's individual needs while maintaining a sense of safety within the relationship. Clearly communicating and establishing boundaries helps reduce anxiety-driven miscommunications while promoting a healthier connection.

8. Navigating Conflict:

Conflict is an inherent part of any relationship, but it becomes particularly challenging in anxious partnerships. Miscommunications can escalate conflicts, as anxious individuals may struggle to articulate their true desires during heated moments. Cultivating conflict resolution techniques, such as active listening, expressing emotions without blame, and finding common ground, can help partners navigate conflicts effectively and unearth their underlying desires.

9. Seeking Professional Help:

If miscommunications and misunderstandings persist, seeking professional help can provide invaluable guidance. Relationship therapists or counselors can assist anxious couples in identifying deep-rooted patterns and offer tools to improve communication and foster healthier relationships. Professional guidance can help decode heart's desires and promote long-lasting emotional security within the relationship.

Decoding heart's desires in anxious relationships requires patience, empathy, and open-mindedness. By recognizing the characteristics of anxiety, communication pitfalls, and the impact of past experiences, anxious partners can strive for more profound connections. Through active listening, fostering empathy, respecting boundaries, and seeking professional assistance when necessary, couples can navigate miscommunications and build stronger relationships based on trust and understanding. Remember, unraveling the complexities of anxious relationships is a journey, and with dedication and effort, it can lead to profound personal growth and fulfillment.

Finding Balance Together: Strategies for Addressing Partner Anxiety

In every relationship, challenges are bound to arise, and one common challenge that many couples face is dealing with partner anxiety. Anxiety can cast a shadow over a person's life, affecting their emotions, thoughts, and behaviors. When one partner in a relationship experiences anxiety, the impact often extends to their significant other as well. However, navigating this delicate situation and finding a balance can be achieved through understanding, communication, and supportive strategies. In this chapter, we will explore the dynamics of partner anxiety and provide valuable strategies for both partners to address and manage anxiety together.

Understanding Partner Anxiety

Anxiety is a complex phenomenon that can manifest differently in each individual. It is crucial to acknowledge that anxiety disorders are medical conditions and not a matter of personal weakness or character flaws. By understanding anxiety and its impact on your partner, you will be better equipped to support them effectively. Here are some essential points to consider:

1. Education: Educate yourself about anxiety disorders by reading

reliable resources, seeking professional advice, or attending support groups. This knowledge will provide a foundation for offering empathetic support to your partner.

2. Communication: Foster open and honest communication about anxiety-related experiences, triggers, and coping mechanisms. Let your partner know that you are there to listen without judgment or criticism.

3. Empathy and Validation: Show understanding and empathy for your partner's emotions and experiences. Validate their feelings rather than dismissing or downplaying them. Remember, anxiety can be overwhelming, and your support can make a significant difference.

4. Establish Boundaries: While it is crucial to be there for your partner, it is equally important to establish healthy boundaries. Creating space for both partners to engage in self-care and maintain individual identities can positively impact the relationship.

Supportive Strategies for the Partner with Anxiety

Supporting your partner in managing their anxiety can be challenging at times. By implementing certain strategies, you can foster a supportive and nurturing environment. Here are some helpful approaches:

1. Encourage Professional Help: With the guidance of a mental health professional, your partner can learn effective coping strategies and develop skills to manage their anxiety better. Encourage them gently, emphasizing that seeking professional help is a sign of strength.

2. Empowerment through Self-Care: Encourage your partner to establish a self-care routine that suits their needs. Activities like exercise, meditation, adequate sleep, and engaging in hobbies can alleviate anxiety symptoms and promote emotional well-being.

3. Be a Calming Presence: Learning to be a calm and grounding force during anxious episodes can provide immense support for your partner. Practice deep breathing exercises together and offer reassurance and comfort during periods of heightened anxiety.

4. Encourage Healthy Lifestyle Habits: Ensure that your partner maintains a balanced diet, exercises regularly, and gets enough rest. These habits contribute to overall well-being and can play a significant role in reducing anxiety symptoms.

5. Normalize Anxiety in the Relationship: Help your partner understand that anxiety is a shared challenge and not an individual burden. By reframing anxiety as something you both face together, you can reduce the feeling of isolation and encourage effective teamwork.

Partner's Self-Care and Coping Strategies

Supporting a partner with anxiety requires taking care of your own well-being as well. Caring for yourself will enable you to be a stable and effective support system. Here are some self-care strategies for partners:

1. Seek Support for Yourself: Reach out to friends, family, or professionals to discuss your experiences and emotions, ensuring you have a support network to rely on. This can help alleviate any emotional burden you may feel.

2. Practice Mindfulness and Stress Reduction Techniques: Incorporate mindfulness exercises or stress-reducing activities into your routine. This can include yoga, meditation, deep breathing, or engaging in hobbies that bring you joy.

3. Establish Communication Rituals: Set aside regular times to discuss your relationship dynamics, emotional well-being, and any concerns you may have. Open and honest communication can help strengthen your bond and address any issues that arise.

4. Personal Boundaries: Recognize and communicate your own needs within the relationship. Establishing healthy boundaries ensures that you have time and space to take care of your own emotional and physical well-being.

5. Educate Yourself: Continue to learn about anxiety, its causes, and coping mechanisms. By educating yourself further, you can enhance your ability to support your partner effectively.

Addressing partner anxiety is not a simple task, but with understanding, empathy, and proactive strategies, couples can find balance together. Remember, you are both on the same team, and by working together, you can create a supportive and loving relationship despite the challenges anxiety may present. By continuing to educate yourselves, seeking professional help, practicing self-care, and establishing boundaries, you can build a foundation of trust and love that helps navigate anxiety's ups and downs.

Beyond Blame: Avoiding Resentment and Building Understanding

In a world where conflicts seem to be omnipresent, it is easy to fall into the trap of blaming others for our misfortunes and misunderstandings. Blame often escalates resentment, causing deeper divisions between individuals and communities. However, by adopting a mindset that goes beyond blame, we can foster understanding, compassion, and ultimately work towards meaningful resolutions. This chapter aims to explore the destructive nature of blame, examine its root causes, and present strategies to cultivate empathy and understanding instead.

The Origins of Blame:

Blame is a natural response when we encounter challenges or conflicts. As social beings, we possess an innate drive to understand and assign responsibility for the outcomes we experience. Unfortunately, this inclination can often cloud our judgment and prevent us from seeing the broader picture. Instead of seeking understanding, blame places us in a defensive stance, hindering any possibility of reconciliation or growth.

Blame is rooted in our need for control and self-preservation. When faced with adversity, we tend to divert attention away from ourselves by pointing fingers at others. This defensive mechanism protects our ego, allowing us to maintain the illusion of security and innocence. However, blaming others rarely alleviates our pain or resolves the underlying issues. Rather, it perpetuates a cycle of resentment, hindering our ability to foster healthy relationships and personal growth.

The Destructive Effects of Blame:

Blame is a powerful force that can have devastating effects on both individuals and communities. At the personal level, it can lead to bitterness, simmering resentment, and a breakdown in communication with loved ones. Strained relationships, tarnished reputations, and a decline in mental well-being often follow. Furthermore, blame can create a culture of hostility and divisiveness, perpetuating conflicts on a societal scale. To break this cycle, it is essential to understand the destructive consequences of blame and actively seek alternative approaches.

Cultivating Understanding:

To move beyond blame and towards understanding, we must embark on a journey of self-awareness and empathy. This process begins with an acknowledgment of our own fallibility and understanding that everyone makes mistakes—ourselves included.

By recognizing our shared vulnerability, we can approach conflicts with humility and compassion, opening doors for dialogue and mutual growth.

Active listening is another vital practice in building understanding. By setting aside our preconceived judgments and genuinely hearing others without interruption, we create space for diverse perspectives and shared insights to emerge. Through active listening, we can bridge the divides that blame creates and uncover common ground for resolution and understanding.

Building empathy is crucial in dismantling the blame game. Empathy allows us to step into another person's shoes, feeling their emotions and experiencing their perspective. By cultivating empathy, we can recognize the complexities of individuals' lives, the influences that shape their behavior, and the challenges they face. This understanding can foster compassion and forgiveness, forging new pathways towards resolution and healing.

Seeking Collaborative Solutions:

Beyond blame lies the opportunity for collaborative problem-solving. Rather than seeking to assign guilt, we can shift our focus to uncovering the root causes of conflicts and working together towards finding solutions. This collaborative mindset breeds synergy and creativity, as diverse ideas and perspectives converge towards a shared objective.

In fostering collaboration, it is vital to maintain open lines of communication. Honest and respectful dialogue enables us to address grievances, voice concerns, and uncover shared goals. By recognizing that conflict can be an opportunity for growth, we can harness its energy to foster transformation and build stronger, more resilient relationships.

Blame is a common yet destructive response to conflicts. Its inherent focus on assigning fault leads to resentment and hinders growth on individual and societal levels. By shifting towards understanding, empathy, and collaborative problem-solving, we can break free from the blame game. This paradigm shift allows us to approach conflicts with openness and curiosity, ultimately leading to healthier relationships, personal growth, and collective transformation. Only then can we truly create a world that thrives on understanding and compassionate connections.

Chapter 5: Practical Steps to Calm the Heart's Storms

In the journey of life, the heart often encounters storms that shake its peace and tranquility. These storms can be triggered by a variety of situations, such as setbacks, stress, conflict, or loss. When our hearts are in turmoil, it becomes crucial to find practical steps that can empower us to navigate these storms with resilience and calmness. This chapter explores a range of effective strategies and proven techniques to help you calm the storms within your heart, restore peace, and find solace amidst the chaos.

Understanding the Storm:

Before we embark on the journey of finding practical steps to calm the heart's storms, it is important to gain a deeper understanding of the storms themselves. A storm in the heart is not just a passing emotional turmoil; it is a profound disturbance that affects our physical, mental, and spiritual well-being. Just as a strong wind blows away the leaves from a tree, heart storms can swiftly uproot our sense of stability and security. Therefore, it is crucial to acknowledge the gravity of these storms and approach them with utmost compassion and care.

1. Cultivating Self-awareness:

The first step towards calming the heart's storms is cultivating self-awareness. Take time to acknowledge and identify the emotions and thoughts that are contributing to your inner turmoil. Understand that it is okay to feel overwhelmed or distressed, as these are natural responses to life's challenges. By recognizing and accepting your emotions, you can take charge of your inner landscape and begin the transformative process of finding peace.

2. Engaging in Mindful Practice:

Mindfulness is a powerful tool that can act as an anchor in stormy moments. Engaging in mindful practices such as meditation, deep breathing exercises, or yoga helps calm the mind and connect with the present moment. These practices allow you to detach from the turbulence within and create a space for inner tranquility to emerge. Even a few minutes of daily mindfulness can have a profound impact on your ability to weather the storms of life.

3. Seeking Support and Connection:

In times of turmoil, seeking support from loved ones or professionals can provide immense solace and strength. Share your burdens with those you trust and allow them to lend an empathetic ear. This act of vulnerability does not weaken you; instead, it opens up avenues for healing and enables you to access the power of human connection. Remember, you are not alone in your struggles, and reaching out for support is a sign of courage and resilience.

4. Embracing Acceptance:

One of the most challenging yet transformative steps in calming the heart's storms is embracing acceptance. Acceptance does not mean giving up or resigning to a fate; rather, it involves acknowledging the reality of the situation and allowing yourself to surrender to it. By accepting the storms within, you can focus your energy on finding constructive solutions rather than being consumed by resistance and negativity.

5. Nurturing Gratitude:

Gratitude has the power to transform even the darkest storms into opportunities for growth and healing. Practice cultivating gratitude by acknowledging the blessings and lessons that come your way, regardless of the circumstances. Reflecting on the positive aspects of your life can help shift your mindset, providing a refreshing perspective that brings peace and restores faith.

6. Engaging in Self-care:

In times of turmoil, self-care should become a priority. Engage in activities that nourish your mind, body, and soul. Whether it's indulging in a relaxing bath, going for a walk in nature, reading a book, or engaging in a hobby, self-care acts as a sanctuary amid the storms. By consciously allocating time and energy for self-care, you empower yourself to face the challenges with resilience and strength.

7. Cultivating a Growth Mindset:

Adopting a growth mindset allows you to view storms as opportunities for personal growth and development. Embrace challenges as lessons that shape your character and build resilience. Understand that setbacks are not failures; they are stepping stones towards reaching your full potential. By aligning your mindset with growth, you can transform storms into catalysts for personal transformation.

Calmness and peace within the heart are not distant dreams; they are within our reach even amidst life's storms. By following these practical steps and finding the ones that resonate with you, you can begin the journey of calming the heart's storms and rediscovering your inner strength. Remember, storms may rage, but within you lies the power to find solace, restore peace, and embrace the serenity that awaits beyond the turmoil.

Self-awareness Soothes: Introspective Techniques for Relationship Anxiety

We all desire healthy and fulfilling relationships, but anxiety can often undermine our ability to fully enjoy them. Relationship anxiety can arise from various sources, such as past experiences, fear of rejection, or even our own insecurities. However, by cultivating self-awareness and using introspective techniques, we can alleviate the burdens of relationship anxiety and create stronger connections with our partners. In this chapter, we will explore various introspective techniques that can help us understand ourselves better and develop healthier relationships. So, let's embark on this transformative journey of self-discovery.

Understanding Relationship Anxiety:

Before delving into the introspective techniques, it is crucial to develop a comprehensive understanding of relationship anxiety. This form of anxiety can manifest as excessive worry, fear of abandonment, or a constant need for reassurance. It can hinder communication, trust, and overall relationship satisfaction. Relationship anxiety often stems from unresolved personal issues, such as low self-esteem, attachment styles, and past traumatic experiences. By acknowledging and accepting the presence of relationship anxiety, we can begin the healing process.

1. Mindfulness Meditation:

Mindfulness meditation is a powerful introspective technique that can help alleviate relationship anxiety. By practicing mindfulness, we develop an awareness of our thoughts, emotions, and bodily sensations without judgment. Through regular meditation sessions, we can observe our anxious thoughts as passing events rather than absolute truths, allowing us to detach from them. This newfound detachment enables us to respond to relationship situations with clarity and compassion, rather than reacting impulsively out of fear.

2. Journaling for Self-Reflection:

Journaling is an effective tool for self-reflection that can offer deep insights into our relationship anxieties. Carve out some time each day to write down your thoughts, feelings, and fears related to your relationships. Explore the patterns that emerge, various triggers, and any recurring themes. Are there any moments or experiences that have intensified your anxiety? Identifying these patterns allows us to gain a better understanding of our triggers and helps us engage in open and honest conversations with our partners.

3. Exploring Attachment Styles:

Attachment styles significantly influence the way we perceive and navigate relationships. Understanding your attachment style can provide valuable insights into your relationship anxiety. The three primary attachment styles are secure, anxious, and avoidant. Secure individuals have a strong sense of self-worth, trust, and healthy independence. Anxious individuals seek excessive reassurance and fear abandonment, while avoidant individuals value independence, often distancing themselves emotionally. By recognizing your attachment style and how it affects your relationship anxiety, you can work towards developing a more secure attachment style, promoting healthier relationships.

4. Cognitive Restructuring:

Another introspective technique to tackle relationship anxiety is cognitive restructuring. This technique involves identifying and challenging negative thought patterns that perpetuate anxiety. We often engage in catastrophic thinking, imagining worst-case scenarios and dwelling on negative possibilities. By challenging these thoughts and replacing them with more rational and positive alternatives, we can reframe our perception of relationship situations. Cognitive restructuring allows us to build a healthier mindset and confront our anxiety with a more realistic perspective.

5. Exploring Personal Values and Boundaries:

Clarifying personal values and setting healthy boundaries is essential for managing relationship anxiety. By identifying your values, you can consciously align your actions and behaviors in a way that promotes your well-being and strengthens your relationships. Similarly, establishing boundaries allows you to protect yourself, communicate your needs, and maintain healthy limits within your relationships. Recognizing and respecting both your own and your partner's boundaries fosters a sense of security, significantly reducing relationship anxiety.

6. Seeking Professional Support:

In certain cases, professional support can be instrumental in navigating relationship anxiety. A trained therapist can provide guidance, support, and additional introspective techniques tailored to your specific needs. Therapy allows for a safe space to explore your anxieties and fears, empowering you with the necessary tools to build healthier relationships. Seeking professional support demonstrates a profound commitment to your personal growth and the well-being of your relationships.

In this chapter, we have explored several introspective techniques for managing relationship anxiety. Cultivating self-awareness is essential in understanding the roots of our fears and insecurities, enabling us to develop healthier relationships. Whether through mindfulness meditation, journaling, exploring attachment styles, cognitive restructuring, clarifying personal values and boundaries, or seeking professional support, each technique offers a unique path towards self-discovery and growth. By practicing these introspective techniques regularly, we can soothe our relationship anxieties and pave the way for more fulfilling and harmonious connections. Remember, the journey of introspection is continuous, and the rewards of self-awareness are immeasurable. Embrace this transformative journey, and may it bring you closer to the lasting love and happiness you deserve.

Therapy and the Turbulent Heart: Professional Help for Anxiety in Relationships

In the realm of human connections, relationships bring both joy and challenges. While love, trust, and support can uplift us, they also have the potential to trigger anxiety. The turbulent heart, riddled with fears and uncertainties, can wreak havoc on our well-being and the harmony of our partnerships. Fortunately, therapy provides a safe haven for individuals grappling with anxiety in relationships. In this chapter, we will delve into the importance of seeking professional help in navigating the complexities of emotional distress found within intimate connections.

Understanding Anxiety in Relationships

Before we explore the therapeutic approach to treating anxiety in relationships, it is crucial to comprehend the roots of this emotional turmoil. Anxiety in relationships often stems from deep-seated insecurities, fear of abandonment, past traumas, or an unhealthy attachment style - all of which we will explore further in upcoming sections.

Insecurity and Fear of Abandonment

At the core of relationship anxiety lies insecurity, an innate human emotion that can wreak havoc on our well-being. Insecurity often manifests as a fear of not being good enough for our partner or a constant worry that they will leave us. This fear of abandonment may stem from past experiences where we felt rejected or betrayed, leading to an amplified sensitivity to signs of potential rejection in present relationships.

Past Traumas and Their Impact

Another significant factor contributing to anxiety in relationships is unresolved past traumas. Traumatic experiences, such as a toxic relationship or emotional/physical abuse, can leave lasting scars that impact our capacity to trust and form healthy attachments. These traumas can act as triggers, resurfacing feelings of fear, insecurity, and vulnerability, even in seemingly secure relationships.

Attachment Styles and Their Influence

Our attachment styles, developed in childhood, greatly influence how we engage with our partners in romantic relationships. Anxious attachment, characterized by a constant need for reassurance and an excessive fear of abandonment, can lead to chronic relationship anxiety. On the other hand, avoidant attachment stems from a fear of intimacy and a tendency to push others away emotionally, often leading to conflicting feelings and heightened anxiety.

The Role of Therapy

Therapy provides a safe and supportive environment to explore and address the anxieties that can plague relationships. By working with a professional, individuals can uncover the root causes of their anxiety, develop coping mechanisms, and acquire tools to build healthier and more fulfilling connections.

Types of Therapy for Relationship Anxiety

1. Cognitive Behavioral Therapy (CBT)

CBT is an evidence-based approach that focuses on identifying and altering negative thought patterns and behaviors. By challenging and reframing irrational beliefs, individuals can rewire their thinking to reduce anxiety and break free from harmful relationship patterns. Therapists guide clients in developing healthier coping strategies, enabling them to respond to relationship fears more effectively.

2. Psychodynamic Therapy

Psychodynamic therapy dives deep into the subconscious mind, searching for hidden motivations and unresolved conflicts that contribute to relationship anxiety. By exploring early life experiences, therapists help individuals uncover patterns and make connections between past traumas and current anxieties. The insights gained from psychodynamic therapy allow individuals to heal, introspect, and create healthier relationship dynamics.

3. EMDR Therapy

Eye Movement Desensitization and Reprocessing (EMDR) therapy is particularly effective for individuals with anxiety stemming from trauma. Through guided eye movements, bilateral stimulation, or tactile taps, EMDR helps reprocess traumatic memories and reduces the emotional charge associated with them. By integrating traumatic experiences, individuals can transform their relationship anxieties and build healthier connections.

4. Emotionally Focused Therapy (EFT)

Emotionally Focused Therapy (EFT) helps couples address relationship anxieties together. A skilled therapist guides partners in exploring their emotional needs, fears, and communication patterns. Through this process, couples learn to build secure attachment bonds, foster empathy, and improve emotional intimacy. EFT enables partners to create a safe haven in their relationship, reducing anxiety and growing together.

The Therapeutic Journey: From Anxiety to Authentic Connections

The road to healing relationship anxiety through therapy is not a quick fix but rather a transformative journey. Healing and growth require dedication, vulnerability, and an acknowledgment of personal responsibility.

Identifying and Acknowledging Anxiety

The first step toward healing is recognizing and accepting the presence of anxiety within oneself and the impact it has on relationships. Acknowledgment allows individuals to take ownership of their emotions and take the necessary steps to seek professional help.

Building a Therapeutic Alliance

Developing a trusting and nurturing relationship with a therapist is pivotal for successful therapy outcomes. A skilled therapist creates a non-judgmental space where individuals feel safe exploring their anxieties, traumas, and vulnerabilities. Through empathy, active listening, and personalized strategies, therapists support individuals in their journey toward healing.

Exploring the Root Causes

Therapy offers a unique opportunity to delve deep into the underlying causes of relationship anxiety. By understanding the origins of anxiety, individuals can gain clarity, make connections, and begin the process of healing. This phase may include revisiting past traumas, examining attachment patterns, and challenging deeply ingrained beliefs.

Developing Coping Strategies

Therapy equips individuals with practical coping strategies to alleviate relationship anxiety. Techniques such as deep breathing exercises, grounding techniques, mindfulness, and journaling help manage emotional distress and enhance self-awareness. Therapists also provide guidance on setting healthy boundaries, fostering open communication, and fostering practices of self-care.

Building Resilience and Self-Confidence

While therapy can provide the necessary tools for recovery, ultimately, individuals must cultivate self-confidence and resilience within themselves. Therapists empower individuals to challenge their negative self-perceptions, cultivate self-love, and build a strong support network. By harnessing resilience, individuals can navigate their relationship anxieties and foster authentic connections with their partners.

Anxiety is an unwelcome companion that can intrude upon our relationships, causing turbulence and distress. However, therapy offers a lifeline, providing a path toward healing, growth, and transformative change. By understanding the root causes of anxiety, seeking professional help, and dedicating oneself to the therapeutic journey, individuals can find solace, cultivate authentic connections, and navigate the complexities of relationships with grace and resilience. Remember, seeking support is not a sign of weakness but a courageous step toward building a brighter, more fulfilling future.

Mindfulness and the Heart: Meditation and Grounding Techniques

Mindfulness and meditation have gained tremendous popularity in recent years as effective practices to enhance overall well-being and reduce stress levels. While the benefits of mindfulness are widely discussed, it is important to recognize that the heart plays a significant role in our practice, both in a metaphorical and literal sense. In this chapter, we delve into the connection between mindfulness and the heart, exploring meditation and grounding techniques that allow us to cultivate a profound sense of connection, compassion, and emotional well-being.

The Heart as a Center of Existence:

The heart has long been perceived as a symbol of love, compassion, and emotionality. Beyond its metaphorical significance, however, science has also revealed the physiological importance of the heart. It is not merely an organ responsible for pumping blood but plays a critical role in regulating our emotions and influencing our overall well-being.

Neurocardiology, the study of the heart-brain connection, has provided remarkable insights into the significance of the heart in our daily experiences. Research has shown that the heart possesses its own intricate network of neurons, neurotransmitters, and ganglia, forming a complex communication system with the brain. This connection allows information to flow bidirectionally between the two organs, impacting our emotional states, cognitive functions, and overall health.

With this newfound understanding, it becomes evident that incorporating the heart into mindfulness and meditation practices can deepen our level of self-awareness, emotional regulation, and compassion towards ourselves and others.

Meditation Techniques for Cultivating Heart-Centered Mindfulness:

1. Loving-Kindness Meditation:

Loving-kindness meditation, also known as Metta meditation, is a powerful practice to develop compassion and nurture love towards oneself and others. This technique involves silently repeating specific phrases or mantras intended to evoke feelings of warmth, empathy, and goodwill. It is a practice that cultivates a deep sense of interconnectedness and fosters a compassionate heart.

To begin this meditation, find a comfortable posture, close your eyes, and bring your attention to your heart center. Start by focusing on sensations within your heart, such as the rhythm of your heartbeat or the warmth it generates. Gradually, direct your awareness towards someone you deeply care about, silently repeating phrases like "May you be happy. May you be healthy. May you be safe. May you live with ease." After extending loving-kindness to yourself, progressively expand your focus to include friends, acquaintances, difficult individuals, and eventually all beings on earth.

2. Heart-Feeling Meditation:

Heart-feeling meditation is a practice that invites us to connect with the heart's wisdom and cultivate positive emotions such as love, gratitude, and joy. This technique encourages us to shift our attention away from the mind and into our heart space, allowing us to tap into the inherent wisdom and harmony residing within us.

To practice heart-feeling meditation, sit in a comfortable position with your eyes closed. Begin by taking a few deep breaths, allowing your body to relax and settle into the present moment. Now, focus your awareness on your heart center, envisioning it as a radiant ball of light or an expansive space filled with warmth and love. As you breathe in, imagine inhaling these qualities, filling your entire being with compassion and joy. With each exhale, allow any tension or negativity to leave your body, creating space for even more positive emotions.

Grounding Techniques for Emotional Well-being:

1. Grounding Breath:

Grounding breath is a simple yet powerful technique to bring our attention back to the present moment and reconnect with our bodies when we feel overwhelmed or disconnected. By focusing on the breath and its sensations within the body, we can anchor ourselves in the present and find a sense of stability amidst chaos.

To practice grounding breath, find a comfortable seat or lie down in a quiet space. Close your eyes and take a few deep breaths, allowing your body to relax. Direct your attention to the sensation of your breath as it enters and leaves your body. Notice the feeling of the air passing through your nostrils or the gentle rise and fall of your abdomen with each inhale and exhale. As thoughts or distractions arise, simply acknowledge them without judgment and gently guide your focus back to your breath, grounding yourself in the present moment.

2. Earthing:

Earthing, also known as grounding, involves connecting with the earth's energy to restore balance and reduce stress. This practice recognizes the healing power of nature and encourages us to spend time outdoors, connecting our bodies directly with the earth's surface.

To practice earthing, find a comfortable outdoor spot, whether it be a grassy patch, sandy beach, or lush forest. Remove your shoes and socks to allow direct contact between your bare feet and the ground. Close your eyes, take a few deep breaths, and bring your awareness to the sensation of your feet touching the earth. Feel the texture, temperature, and energy exchange between your body and the ground. As you stand or walk mindfully, absorb the earth's healing energy, allowing it to ground you, induce feelings of calmness, and restore emotional equilibrium.

Mindfulness and the heart are intimately linked, both in a metaphorical and literal sense. By incorporating meditation techniques that focus on the heart's wisdom and cultivating compassion, we can deepen our practice and experience profound emotional well-being. Grounding techniques, such as grounding breath and earthing, allow us to stay rooted in the present moment, fostering stability and reducing stress. Together, these practices pave the way for a more heart-centered mindfulness journey, enabling us to live with greater compassion, empathy, and connectivity to ourselves, others, and the world around us.

Creating Safe Harbors: Building Support Systems Outside the Relationship

When we enter into a romantic relationship, we often believe that our partner will become our everything – our confidant, best friend, and support system. While it is indeed important to foster a deep connection with our significant other, relying solely on them for emotional support may become overwhelming and can potentially strain the relationship. To maintain a healthy and balanced partnership, it is crucial to establish support systems outside the relationship – safe harbors that provide a sense of belonging and security beyond our romantic ties. In this chapter, we will explore the importance of building robust support systems, how to cultivate them, and the numerous benefits they bring to both individuals and their relationships.

The Benefits of External Support Systems

1. Expanding Perspectives:

When we interact with a diverse circle of friends, family, and other individuals outside our relationship, we gain exposure to a broader range of ideas, beliefs, and experiences. This exposure broadens our perspective, allowing us to see the world through different lenses, enhancing our personal growth in the process. Our support systems serve as a constant reminder that we are not alone and that there are multiple viewpoints on various aspects of life.

2. Emotional Outlet:

Humans are complex beings with a wide range of emotions, and it is unrealistic to expect our partners to be our sole emotional outlet. By nurturing relationships beyond our romantic one, we create safe spaces to express ourselves, share our feelings, and seek advice. These external connections provide an opportunity for catharsis, allowing us to unwind, reflect, and gain valuable insights from those who care about us.

3. Accountability:

Having an external support system can help us remain accountable for our actions, goals, and aspirations. Our support network can act as mirrors, reflecting our actions back to us and offering constructive feedback when needed. When we have people who genuinely care about us, they are often willing to call us out when we are falling short of our potential or making choices that are detrimental to our wellbeing, providing an invaluable source of guidance and motivation.

4. Enhanced Relationship Skills:

Nurturing connections outside the relationship helps us develop valuable relationship skills, as we observe and learn from the dynamics of others' interactions. By witnessing various communication styles, conflict resolution techniques, and the give-and-take of healthy relationships, we can bring these learnings into our own romantic lives. The ability to adapt and learn from different relationships allows us to continuously evolve as individuals and partners.

Building Support Systems

1. Identifying Potential Support Networks:
To build robust support systems, it is essential to identify individuals and communities that align with our interests, values, and aspirations. Whether it be close friends, family members, colleagues, or shared interest groups, the key is finding people who genuinely care about our wellbeing and provide a healthy space for growth and connection. It is important to remember that our support system doesn't have to consist of a large number of people; quality over quantity is paramount.

2. Cultivating Genuine Connections:
Establishing authentic connections involves investing time and effort into building and nurturing relationships. Actively engage in conversation, show genuine interest in others' lives, and be available when they need support. Building trust and reciprocity within these connections is crucial. By being reliable and supportive, we set the foundation for long-lasting, meaningful relationships.

3. Diversifying Support Systems:
There are various realms of life where we might seek support, such

as emotional, professional, and recreational. It is essential to diversify our support systems to cater to our diverse needs. This diversification could be achieved by maintaining a balance between friends, mentors, support groups, professional networks, or even seeking professional help like therapists or coaches for specific areas of our lives. By doing so, we ensure that our support networks cover different aspects of our wellbeing.

4. Investing in the Relationships:

Like any relationship, our external support systems require maintenance and nurturing. Regularly check-in with your friends, attend social events, and be present when they need you. Healthy relationships require give-and-take, so be willing to contribute and offer support whenever possible. Remember, building a strong and reliable support system is an ongoing process that requires time, patience, and dedication.

As we conclude this chapter, it's essential to reiterate the importance of building support systems outside our romantic relationships. These external safe harbors provide us with emotional, intellectual, and social connections that can enhance our personal growth and strengthen our partnerships. By embracing diverse perspectives, cultivating genuine connections, and diversifying our support systems, we ensure that we have a solid foundation to navigate life's challenges and triumphs. Building robust support systems not only benefits us as individuals but also contributes to the health and longevity of our romantic relationships.

Chapter 6: Charting a Course to Stronger Bonds

In this fast-paced and ever-evolving world, our personal relationships have become more important than ever. Strong bonds with our loved ones not only provide emotional support but also contribute to our overall well-being and happiness. However, nurturing and maintaining these relationships can be challenging at times. In this chapter, we will explore various strategies for charting a course to stronger bonds, helping you navigate through the ups and downs of building and maintaining healthy and fulfilling connections.

Section 1: Understanding Relationship Dynamics

Before we can begin strengthening our connections with others, it is crucial to understand the dynamics that govern these relationships. In this section, we will delve into the various factors that influence the strength of our bonds.

1.1 Communication: The Foundation of Strong Bonds

Effective communication lies at the heart of any healthy relationship. We will explore the art of active listening, assertiveness, and empathy, helping you enhance your communication skills and foster mutual understanding.

1.2 Trust and Vulnerability

Trust forms the bedrock upon which strong bonds are built. Learning to trust others and be vulnerable ourselves is essential for creating deep connections. We will discuss strategies for building trust, overcoming trust issues, and allowing ourselves to be vulnerable in our relationships.

Section 2: Strengthening Connections

Once we understand the dynamics of relationships, we can move on to actively strengthening our bonds. This section will focus on practical strategies and techniques to improve and reinforce our connections.

2.1 Quality Time: Nurturing Bonds through Quality Interactions

Spending quality time with our loved ones is a precious investment in our relationships. We will explore ways to create meaningful experiences and connections, such as shared activities, open and honest conversations, and focusing on each other's needs.

2.2 Emotional Support: Becoming a Pillar of Strength

Being emotionally available for our loved ones is crucial in times of joy, sorrow, or when they simply need someone to lean on. We will discuss techniques for offering genuine and compassionate emotional support in any situation.

2.3 Managing Conflict: Resolving Differences and Growing Together

Conflict is an inevitable part of any relationship, but how we manage it determines the strength of our bonds. We will examine conflict resolution strategies, including effective communication, active listening, compromise, and forgiveness. Understanding each other's perspectives and finding common ground will allow us to come out of conflicts stronger than ever.

Section 3: Nurturing Relationships from Afar

In our increasingly connected world, maintaining strong bonds with loved ones who are physically distant has become more important than ever. This section will focus on strategies for nurturing long-distance relationships.

3.1 Technology: Enhancing Connection in the Digital Age

Utilizing technology to bridge geographical gaps can greatly contribute to maintaining strong relationships. We will explore various ways to use technology effectively, such as video calls, text messaging, and social media, while also recognizing the limitations of virtual interaction.

3.2 Thoughtfulness and Surprise: Keeping the Spark Alive

Beyond technology, thoughtfulness and surprise play a significant role in nurturing long-distance relationships. We will discuss creative ways to show appreciation, provide emotional support, and keep the spark alive, even from afar.

Strong bonds with our loved ones form the backbone of a fulfilling and joyful life. By understanding the dynamics of relationships, actively working on communication and trust, and nurturing connections through quality time, emotional support, and conflict resolution, we can chart a course to stronger bonds. Additionally, in this digital age, we can use technology thoughtfully to maintain and strengthen long-distance relationships. As we explore these strategies further in the upcoming chapters of this book, remember that nurturing relationships is a lifelong journey that requires time, effort, and dedication.

Communication is Heart's Key: Effective Dialogue Strategies in Relationships

In the intricate tapestry of human relationships, communication serves as the lifeblood that nourishes and sustains connections. Just as a key unlocks a door, effective dialogue strategies hold the power to open hearts and forge meaningful bonds. This chapter explores the essence of communication in relationships, delving into the fundamental principles and practical techniques that can enhance dialogue between individuals. By understanding and implementing these strategies, we can foster understanding, empathy, and harmony, ultimately strengthening the foundation of our relationships.

1. The Core of Communication:

At its core, communication encompasses more than mere verbal exchanges. It involves active listening, understanding non-verbal cues, and empathetically responding to the emotions expressed. To truly connect with others, we must first embark on a deeper exploration of what drives effective communication, unraveling the intricate layers that make it the heart's key.

2. Active Listening: The Power of Presence:

One of the most crucial aspects of effective communication is active listening. True listening involves giving our undivided attention, suspending judgment, and fostering an open mind. By being present in the moment, we can provide a safe space for others to express themselves fully. Engaging in active listening allows us to comprehend not only the words spoken but also the emotions underlying them.

3. Empathy: The Bridge to Understanding:

Building upon active listening, empathy serves as the bridge that links individuals in a relationship. Empathy, the ability to understand and share the feelings of another, allows us to connect on a deeper level, validating and acknowledging the emotions experienced by our loved ones. By embracing empathy, we take an important step toward establishing trust and creating a supportive environment.

4. Non-Verbal Communication: Speaking Without Words:

While words are the foundation of conversation, non-verbal communication represents an equally significant form of expression. Gestures, facial expressions, and body language all play a crucial role in relaying emotions, intentions, and messages. By attuning ourselves to these subtle cues, we can more effectively understand

and respond to the unspoken aspects of communication.

5. Learning and Unlearning: Breaking Down Barriers:

Effective dialogue also requires a willingness to learn and unlearn certain communication habits. By challenging assumptions, biases, and preconceived notions, we open ourselves up to new perspectives, allowing for growth and understanding within our relationships. Through active mental flexibility, we create space for healthy dialogue, avoiding patterns of defensiveness that can hinder communication.

6. Conflict Resolution: Nurturing Growth:

All relationships experience conflicts, and mastering the art of resolving conflicts with effective dialogue is crucial for their sustenance. By utilizing tools such as active listening, empathy, and assertive communication, we can navigate disagreements in a constructive manner. Conflict resolution not only resolves immediate issues but also fosters growth, deepening the bond between individuals.

7. Cultivating Trust and Vulnerability:

Trust acts as the bedrock upon which strong relationships are built. Effective dialogue requires the cultivation of trust, allowing individuals to be vulnerable and authentic in their expression. By creating safe spaces for honest communication, we foster an environment where open dialogue thrives, strengthening emotional connections and laying the groundwork for lasting relationships.

8. Mindful Communication: The Power of Words:

The words we choose have the power to either uplift or wound. Mindful communication involves being conscious of the impact our words can have on others. By practicing kindness, respect, and compassion in our verbal exchanges, we can build bridges rather than walls, ensuring that our message is received in the intended manner.

Communication, as the heart's key, holds immeasurable power in nurturing relationships. By employing strategies such as active listening, empathy, and non-verbal communication, we can traverse the labyrinth of human connections, leading to deeper understanding, compassion, and harmony. Honing these techniques requires practice, patience, and a genuine desire to foster meaningful dialogue. Armed with these skills, we can unlock the true potential of our relationships, unleashing the transformative power of communication on our journey to emotional connection and lasting love.

Rediscovering Passion Amidst Fear: Reigniting Intimacy and Trust

In the realm of intimate relationships, fear can cast a looming shadow over our ability to connect deeply with our partners. Whether derived from past traumas, present insecurities, or the uncertainty of the future, fear has the potential to cripple our ability to embrace passion and nurture trust. However, amidst these challenges, lies an opportunity for growth, an opportunity to reignite intimacy and trust in profound and meaningful ways. In this chapter, we will explore various strategies and insights that can help individuals and couples rediscover passion amidst fear, ultimately nurturing a deeper sense of connection and trust within their relationship.

Unraveling the Threads of Fear:

Before we can begin the journey towards reigniting intimacy and trust, it is imperative to understand the roots of fear within a relationship. Fear can manifest itself in countless ways, often instigating a deep sense of vulnerability and unease. Past relationship traumas, such as infidelity or emotional abuse, can create a reluctance to trust fully. Additionally, personal insecurities and the fear of rejection can hinder our ability to truly open up to our partners, stifling any potential for passion to flourish. Acknowledging and unraveling these threads of fear is the first step towards reigniting intimacy and trust.

1. Cultivating Emotional Safety:

A fundamental aspect of reigniting intimacy is the cultivation of emotional safety within the relationship. When fear takes hold, individuals tend to build walls of self-protection, preventing genuine connection and vulnerability. Creating a safe and non-judgmental space for open communication is paramount. Encouraging active listening, empathy, and a willingness to understand one another's fears and concerns creates a foundation of trust, allowing intimacy to blossom.

2. Healing Past Wounds:

To reignite passion and trust, it is vital to address and heal past relationship wounds. This requires a willingness to confront and process these traumas, with the support of a licensed therapist if needed. Exploring the emotions tied to past experiences, expressing pain, and forgiving both oneself and one's partner are crucial steps towards releasing fear's grip on a relationship. By acknowledging and working through these wounds together, couples can pave the way for deeper intimacy.

3. Embracing Vulnerability:

At the core of reigniting intimacy and trust lies the willingness to embrace vulnerability. Fear often stems from a fear of rejection or judgment, leading individuals to hold back their true selves from their partners. However, it is through vulnerability that couples can truly connect on a profound level. By sharing fears, insecurities, and desires with our partners, we create opportunities for genuine understanding, support, and growth. Embracing vulnerability cultivates a sense of emotional intimacy that reignites the flame of passion within any relationship.

4. Rebuilding Trust:

When trust has been shattered, either through past traumas or recent breaches of trust, the process of rebuilding becomes essential. Rebuilding trust requires transparency, consistency, and a genuine effort to repair the damage caused. This may involve open communication, setting clear expectations, and being accountable for one's actions. Patience, understanding, and practicing forgiveness are key elements in the delicate process of rebuilding trust, allowing both individuals to feel secure and safe within the relationship once again.

5. Cultivating Intimacy:

Intimacy is a multifaceted aspect of any relationship, encompassing emotional, physical, and intellectual connections. When fear permeates the relationship, these facets often suffer, leaving partners feeling disconnected and distant. To reignite intimacy, it is crucial to create shared experiences, engage in meaningful conversations, and allocate quality time for one another. Exploring physical touch, intimacy exercises, and expressing affection can help rekindle passion and deepen the bond between partners.

6. Nurturing Individual Growth:

Fear can often stifle personal growth within a relationship. Rediscovering passion amidst fear requires individuals to focus on their own personal development. By pursuing individual interests, engaging in self-reflective practices, and nurturing personal well-being, individuals can regain a sense of self-confidence and independence. This personal growth not only enriches individual lives but also facilitates a healthier and more passionate connection within the relationship.

As fear permeates our relationships, reigniting passion and trust may seem like a daunting task. However, by unraveling the threads of fear, cultivating emotional safety, healing past wounds, embracing vulnerability, rebuilding trust, and nurturing intimacy and individual growth, couples can begin to rediscover the passion that once thrived within their relationship. This journey towards reigniting intimacy and trust requires patience, perseverance, and a genuine commitment to growth. By taking these steps, couples can create a relationship that transcends fear, and instead, thrives on a deep sense of connection, intimacy, and trust.

Building Bridges: Activities and Rituals to Strengthen Connection

In a world that is becoming increasingly disconnected and divided, it is more important than ever to prioritize building bridges and fostering connections. Whether it is in personal relationships, professional collaborations, or even within communities, creating meaningful connections can enrich our lives and bring about positive change. In this chapter, we will explore a variety of activities and rituals designed to strengthen connections and bridge any gaps that may exist. These activities are versatile and can be applied in various contexts, helping individuals and groups foster a sense of unity and establish deeper relationships.

Activity 1: Shared Storytelling:

Stories have a unique power to captivate us and create a shared experience. By engaging in shared storytelling, individuals can connect on a deeper level and gain insight into each other's perspectives and experiences. This activity can be carried out in a structured format, where participants take turns adding to a story, or informally, where individuals share anecdotes from their lives. The key is to create a safe and non-judgmental space where everyone feels comfortable sharing and listening. This activity can be particularly useful in team-building exercises or community gatherings, allowing individuals to bond over shared narratives.

Activity 2: Appreciation Circle:

In our fast-paced lives, we often forget to express gratitude and appreciation for those around us. The appreciation circle is a simple yet powerful activity that fosters connection and strengthens relationships. Gather a small group of individuals and form a circle. One by one, each participant takes a turn expressing appreciation towards someone else in the circle. This can be done by acknowledging their strengths, expressing gratitude for their support, or recognizing their positive impact. The act of showing appreciation not only deepens connections but also boosts morale and creates an atmosphere of positivity.

Activity 3: Collaborative Art Project:

Art has the potential to transcend language barriers and foster connection between diverse individuals. Engaging in a collaborative art project brings people together, challenging them to work towards a common goal. This activity can be as simple as painting a mural on a community wall or as intricate as creating a mosaic masterpiece. The key is to emphasize teamwork and collaboration, allowing individuals to contribute their unique skills and perspectives. Through this process, participants develop trust, communication skills, and a sense of belonging.

Activity 4: Intercultural Potluck:

Cultivating connections across different cultures can be an enriching experience and broaden our horizons. The intercultural potluck is a delightful activity that encourages individuals to come together and celebrate diversity through food. Each participant is invited to bring a dish from their cultural background, along with the story behind it. This activity promotes dialogue, understanding, and appreciation for different traditions and customs. Sharing meals not only brings people closer but also highlights our commonalities, nourishing both the body and the soul.

Activity 5: Group Volunteering:

Engaging in community service or group volunteering activities can create a sense of unity and purpose among individuals. By working together towards a shared goal, participants develop a sense of camaraderie and learn the value of collective action. This can involve activities such as cleaning up a local park, organizing a fundraising event for a charitable cause, or volunteering at a nearby shelter. Group volunteering not only strengthens connections within the team but also fosters a sense of connection to the broader community.

Ritual 1: Circle of Trust:

The Circle of Trust is a ritual designed to deepen connections and establish a safe and supportive environment. This ritual is particularly useful in professional settings, where individuals may feel hesitant to express vulnerability. Begin by gathering participants in a circle and setting clear guidelines for confidentiality and non-judgment. Then, allow each person to share a personal reflection or concern. With each participant speaking and the group attentively listening, trust is built, bonds are formed, and a sense of belonging is established. This ritual serves as a reminder that everyone's experiences and voices are valued, fostering connections based on trust and authenticity.

Ritual 2: Gratitude Jar:

The Gratitude Jar ritual is a wonderful way to cultivate gratitude and nourish relationships. Each participant is provided with a small jar and a collection of colorful slips of paper. Over a defined period, such as a week or a month, participants are encouraged to write down moments, experiences, or individuals they are grateful for. Once a day, individuals can add their gratitude notes to their jars. At the end of the designated time frame, participants gather together to read aloud their gratitude notes, expressing their appreciation for one another. This ritual strengthens connections by highlighting the positive aspects of each individuals' presence in each other's lives. In a world that often seems divided and disconnected, building bridges and fostering connections is a vital endeavor. The activities and rituals mentioned in this chapter serve as tools to bring people closer, encourage understanding, and establish a sense of unity. By engaging in shared storytelling, practicing appreciation, collaborating on art projects, celebrating diversity through intercultural potlucks, or engaging in group volunteering, individuals can strengthen their relationships, both personal and professional. Additionally, rituals such as the Circle of Trust and the Gratitude Jar provide structured frameworks for deepening connections and nurturing gratitude. By incorporating these activities and rituals into our lives, we can contribute to a more connected and compassionate world.

Committing to Heart's Growth: The Role of Commitment in Overcoming Relationship Anxiety

In the world of romantic relationships, anxiety can often take hold, leaving individuals feeling trapped in a web of doubt and insecurity. Relationship anxiety can manifest in various forms, such as fear of abandonment, excessive jealousy, or even a constant need for reassurance. While these anxieties can be overwhelming, it is crucial to remember that they are not insurmountable. This chapter explores the significance of commitment in overcoming relationship anxiety, providing insights into how a steadfast dedication to personal growth can lead to healthier, more fulfilling connections.

Understanding Relationship Anxiety:

Before delving into the role of commitment, it is essential to comprehend the underlying causes and symptoms of relationship anxiety. Often, this anxiety stems from past experiences that have shaped our beliefs about love and trust. Perhaps we have encountered infidelity, abandonment, or rejection in previous relationships, leading us to question our own worthiness of love and causing us to doubt our partners' intentions.

Insecurities and fears can manifest themselves in various ways. For instance, someone plagued by relationship anxiety might excessively seek reassurance, constantly doubting their partner's fidelity or developing irrational jealousies. They may fear being abandoned or rejected, causing them to engage in clingy behavior or constantly play out worst-case scenarios in their minds. All these anxious thoughts and behaviors can take a significant toll on both the individual experiencing them and their relationship as a whole.

The Role of Commitment:

Commitment acts as a powerful antidote to relationship anxiety, offering a pathway towards growth and emotional stability. When we commit to a relationship, we embrace the willingness to face our fears, confront insecurities, and address the root causes of our anxieties. This commitment is not solely about commitment to our partners; it is primarily a commitment to ourselves and our personal growth.

1. Commitment to Self-Reflection:

Overcoming relationship anxiety begins with self-reflection. It requires introspection and a willingness to explore our past experiences and their impact on our present fears. By committing to self-reflection, we gain insight into the patterns and behaviors that contribute to our anxieties. Whether through therapy, journaling, or seeking guidance from trusted mentors, embarking on this journey of self-discovery allows us to develop a better understanding of ourselves, our triggers, and our emotional vulnerabilities.

2. Commitment to Communication:

Effective communication is the lifeblood of any relationship. When overcoming relationship anxiety, it becomes even more crucial. Committing to open and honest communication with our partners creates a safe space for dialogue, understanding, and vulnerability. By expressing our fears and insecurities, we allow our partners to support us, debunk unfounded assumptions, and foster deeper levels of trust. This commitment to communication paves the way for emotional growth and the healing of past wounds.

3. Commitment to Personal Growth:

Personal growth is an ongoing process that requires commitment, dedication, and self-compassion. By committing to our own growth, we actively work towards healing our anxieties. This can involve engaging in activities that enhance self-esteem, investing in self-care, or seeking professional help. Embracing personal growth empowers us to make positive changes in our lives, reframe negative beliefs, and build a strong foundation of self-love. Through this commitment, we not only overcome relationship anxiety but also foster a sense of security and well-being that enriches all aspects of our lives.

4. Commitment to Trust:

Trust is the cornerstone of any successful relationship. But for individuals grappling with relationship anxiety, trust can feel elusive and fragile. Committing to trust involves an intentional effort to challenge negative thoughts and replace them with more positive and realistic beliefs. It requires acknowledging that not all partners are the same and that our present relationship is an opportunity for a new beginning. As we commit to trust, we allow ourselves to be vulnerable, enabling love and connection to flourish.

Committing to heart's growth is a transformative journey that can help individuals overcome the limitations imposed by relationship anxiety. By dedicating ourselves to self-reflection, communication, personal growth, and trust, we pave the way for healing, growth, and more fulfilling connections.

The role of commitment in overcoming relationship anxiety cannot be understated. It is a testament to our resilience and capacity for growth. By embracing commitment, we empower ourselves to rewrite the narratives of our past, fostering love, trust, and emotional well-being. Remember, commitment is not about finding the perfect relationship; it is about growing into the best version of ourselves and embarking on a journey towards a fulfilling and anxiety-free love.

Chapter 7: Embracing the Journey of the Heart

As we continue our exploration into the depths of the human experience, we find ourselves at a critical juncture on our journey. Chapter 7 marks a turning point, a moment where we dive into the realm of emotions, passion, and the extraordinary power of the human heart. It is here that we learn to embrace the beauty and complexity of our emotions, and discover the transformative potential they hold.

In our modern society, we often find ourselves overwhelmed by the relentless noise of the external world. We build walls around our hearts, shielding ourselves from vulnerability, fearing the immense power that emotions can unleash within us. However, deep within our essence, lies an untapped wellspring of emotions, just waiting to be acknowledged and embraced.

To embark on this journey of the heart, we must first confront our fears and face the darkness that lies within. It is through this process of self-discovery that we begin to unravel the threads of our emotions, casting aside the mask of indifference we wear in the world. By embracing our vulnerabilities, we open ourselves up to a world of profound love, joy, and fulfillment. It is an invitation to embrace our true essence and connect with others on a deeply human level.

The journey of the heart is not a linear path; it is a dance of light and shadow, joy and sorrow. In Chapter 7, we explore the spectrum of emotions that color our lives, understanding that each emotion serves a purpose in our growth and evolution. We delve into the exhilaration of love, the anguish of grief, the fires of passion, and the tranquility of peace. Through this exploration, we learn that emotions are not to be feared, but rather welcomed as teachers and catalysts for personal growth.

Love, the most profound emotion of all, takes center stage in this chapter. We traverse the landscape of romantic love, familial love, and platonic love, recognizing the unique qualities each relationship brings into our lives. Love has the power to heal, to transform, and to ignite a spark within us that sets our souls ablaze. It is through love that we experience the deepest connections with others, transcending the boundaries of time and space.

Yet, love does not come without its challenges. In our pursuit of love, we often stumble upon heartbreak, disappointment, and loss. Chapter 7 brings us face to face with these experiences, encouraging us to turn inward and cultivate resilience. We learn that heartbreak is not a sign of weakness but a testament to our capacity to love deeply. It is through the process of healing that we discover our inner strength and the power of self-love.

Passion, too, plays a pivotal role in the journey of the heart. It is the irresistible force that propels us forward, fueling our dreams and igniting our purpose. In Chapter 7, we explore the ways in which passion can inspire us to live a life of authenticity and meaning. We learn to follow the whispers of our hearts, casting aside societal expectations and embracing our unique passions. Through passion, we tap into our creative potential and become creators of our own destinies.

As we embrace the journey of the heart, we also encounter the depths of sorrow and grief. Life is an intricate tapestry woven with both joy and pain, and Chapter 7 recognizes the importance of sitting with our grief, honoring the losses we have endured. Grief is not something to be rushed or suppressed; it is a necessary process of healing and growth. By leaning into our sorrows, we allow space for transformation, finding solace in the understanding that life and loss are inextricably linked.

By the end of Chapter 7, we come to understand that our emotions are not to be tamed or controlled but rather embraced and integrated into our lives. The human heart is a vast ocean where waves of emotion ebb and flow, each carrying a unique lesson for us to learn. As we embark on this journey, we learn to surf these waves, finding balance and harmony amidst the ever-changing tides.

Through embracing the journey of the heart, we not only forge deeper connections with ourselves but also with the world around us. We recognize that emotion is the common thread that binds humanity together, reminding us of our shared humanity beneath the surface of our differences. It is through the power of our hearts that we find compassion, empathy, and understanding, ultimately creating a more harmonious and loving world.

Chapter 7 invites you to embark on this transformative journey, where the heart takes center stage. It urges you to cast aside your fears, shed the layers of protection, and dare to expose your vulnerabilities. In surrendering to the sacred and mysterious dance of emotions, you will find the courage to embrace your true essence, unearthing the limitless potential that lies within your heart's embrace.

So, my dear fellow traveler, take a deep breath, and let us embark on this soul-stirring odyssey together. The journey of the heart awaits, filled with both beauty and challenges, joy and sorrow. As we navigate its depths, we will discover a world where emotions reign supreme, painting our lives with vibrant hues and transforming us into beings of love, resilience, and extraordinary authenticity.

Lessons from Heart's Pasts: Reflecting on Past Challenges and Growth

Life is a journey filled with both joyous moments and heart-wrenching experiences. Throughout this tumultuous journey, our hearts go through a myriad of challenges that shape us into the individuals we are today. In this chapter, we will delve into the lessons gleaned from our heart's pasts, reflecting upon the obstacles we have faced and the growth garnered from these challenges.

Chapter 1: Unrequited Love - A Lesson in Self-Love

Love has the power to awaken the deepest emotions within us, but it can also present itself as an unyielding force, leaving us exposed and vulnerable. Unrequited love, in particular, has an uncanny ability to penetrate our soul, teaching us the importance of self-love. Through heartache and longing, we learn to prioritize our own well-being, setting boundaries, and nourishing our inner selves.

Chapter 2: Betrayal - Understanding the Complexity of Trust

Betrayal shatters our notion of security, leaving us questioning the authenticity of our relationships. As wounded as we may be after experiencing betrayal, it is through this pain that we uncover the importance of trust in our lives. We learn to navigate the intricacies of human nature, realizing that while trust can be fragile, it is an essential ingredient for genuine connections.

Chapter 3: Heartbreak - Embracing Grief and Resilience

Heartbreak takes many forms, leaving its mark upon our souls and forever altering our understanding of love. In these moments of intense pain, we are forced to confront our deepest fears, acknowledging the fragility of our hearts. Through the healing process, we learn to be gentle with ourselves, allowing grief to guide us towards resilience and a newfound sense of strength.

Chapter 4: Loss and Mourning - Embracing the Circle of Life

Loss is an inevitable part of the human experience, and mourning is the necessary process that accompanies it. Whether grieving the loss of a loved one or the end of a chapter in our lives, we come to understand the inherent vulnerability of our hearts. Through the pain, we acquire an appreciation for the intricacies of life and the transient nature of our existence, teaching us to treasure the present moment.

Chapter 5: Forgiveness - Liberating the Heart

Forgiveness is a powerful act that has the potential to set us free from the shackles of anger, hurt, and resentment. It is through forgiving others that we learn the art of compassion, cultivating empathy and understanding. As our hearts open to forgiveness, we embark on a journey of liberation, releasing ourselves from the burden of pain and embracing the path of healing.

Chapter 6: Self-Discovery – The Compassionate Heart

The process of self-discovery is often accompanied by deep introspection, as we navigate the depths of our emotions and question our core beliefs. Through retrospection, we unearth our true passions, values, and desires, allowing our hearts to guide us towards a life filled with authenticity and purpose. This chapter explores the profound wisdom gained by embracing the journey of self-discovery.

Chapter 7: Transformation - Evolving Into Our Authentic Selves

Life is a continuous cycle of growth and transformation. The heart learns from its past, acquiring invaluable lessons that pave the way for personal evolution. Through embracing change, we shed our old selves and step into the realm of authenticity, experiencing profound liberation and a heightened sense of fulfillment.

The lessons woven across our heart's pasts intricately shape who we become as individuals. Through countless challenges, heartaches, and moments of growth, we emerge stronger, wiser, and more compassionate. It is through reflection and introspection that we cultivate a deep understanding of the profound lessons that our hearts have learned, allowing us to navigate future challenges with grace and resilience. As we reflect on our past experiences, we pave the way for a heart-centered future, filled with growth, love, and boundless possibilities.

Future Horizons: Envisioning a Future Free from Crippling Anxiety

In this chapter, we delve into a world where crippling anxiety is alleviated, and individuals can envision a future free from its shackles. We explore the potential future landscapes of mental health, examining emerging technologies, therapies, and societal changes that may contribute to a world liberated from the grips of anxiety disorders. While our exploration is rooted in the realm of imagination, it is driven by the desire to inspire hope and spur innovation to advance mental health care. Join us as we embark on a journey to envision a future where anxiety no longer holds us back and where anyone can thrive.

Section 1: Embracing Technological Innovation

1.1 Virtual Reality Therapy: Creating Safe Spaces

Imagine a world where virtual reality (VR) technology becomes an integral part of anxiety treatment. With VR therapy, individuals can safely confront their fears and phobias in a controlled environment. Whether it's fear of heights, socializing, or public speaking, VR therapy creates immersive simulations that expose patients gradually to their anxieties, helping them build resilience and overcome their fears. Furthermore, the advancements in haptic feedback technology provide a realistic and interactive experience, activating additional senses to make the therapy even more effective.

1.2 Artificial Intelligence as Support

Artificial intelligence (AI) has the potential to revolutionize mental health care. Imagine having a personal AI assistant that provides intelligent insights, offering emotional support, and helping individuals manage their anxiety symptoms. These AI companions can detect patterns of anxiety through voice and facial recognition, providing tailored coping mechanisms and strategies. By leveraging machine learning algorithms, they can continuously learn and adapt to an individual's needs, offering personalized interventions and effectively adapting to crisis situations.

Section 2: Holistic Approaches to Mental Well-Being

2.1 Mindfulness and Meditation

Embracing mindfulness and meditation as core components of mental health strategies is integral to the future landscape of anxiety treatment. In our increasingly fast-paced and stressful world, enabling individuals to cultivate awareness and focus on the present moment is paramount. Schools, workplaces, and other institutions prioritize incorporating mindfulness practices into their daily routines, thereby creating a culture of emotional intelligence, resilience, and reduced anxiety.

2.2 Integrative Therapies

The future envisions a holistic approach to treating anxiety, integrating traditional therapies with alternative practices. Music therapy, art therapy, and animal-assisted therapy are just a few examples of integrative therapies that offer unique ways to manage anxiety. By leveraging the therapeutic potential of these practices, individuals can tap into their innate creativity, connect with nature, and experience the healing power of human-animal bonds.

Section 3: Building Supportive Environments

3.1 Redefining Success

In a future free from crippling anxiety, societal norms shift, embracing a broader definition of success. The emphasis moves away from material wealth and external achievements, towards a focus on well-being, fulfillment, and connection. By fostering supportive environments that prioritize mental health and encourage work-life balance, the pressures that contribute to anxiety diminish, enabling individuals to flourish.

3.2 Promoting Emotional Literacy

Imagine a world where emotional intelligence is taught and valued from an early age. Schools invest in comprehensive emotional literacy programs, ensuring children learn to identify and manage their feelings with ease. The integration of emotional intelligence into educational and professional systems equips individuals with the skills needed to navigate the complexities of life, reducing anxiety triggers and promoting overall well-being.

Section 4: Destigmatizing Mental Health

4.1 Breaking Barriers

In the future, society embraces mental health as an essential component of overall well-being. Stigma surrounding mental health is challenged and dismantled through open conversations, public awareness campaigns, and widespread education. Mental health care becomes universally accessible, removing barriers to treatment and empowering individuals to seek help without fear of judgment or discrimination.

4.2 Embracing Peer Support

Peer support networks become a cornerstone of the mental health landscape. In a future free from anxiety, individuals connect with others who share similar experiences, providing a sense of belonging, empathy, and understanding. Online communities, support groups, and mentorship programs flourish, offering spaces for growth, healing, and shared wisdom.

As we envision a future free from crippling anxiety, it becomes clear that achieving these horizons requires a collaborative effort from all sectors of society. This exploration of future possibilities is intended to ignite innovation, inspire action, and fuel the collective ambition to address anxiety disorders comprehensively. By embracing emerging technologies, embracing holistic approaches, nurturing supportive environments, and destigmatizing mental health, we can forge a future where anxiety is no longer an impediment to collective flourishing. Let us continue our quest towards a world where all individuals can envision a future free from the crippling grip of anxiety.

Community and Heart: Seeking Support from Others on a Similar Journey

Life can be a roller coaster ride with countless ups and downs. As we navigate through its twists and turns, there are times when the weight of our burdens feels overwhelming, leaving us yearning for solace and understanding. In such vulnerable moments, seeking support from others on a similar journey can provide us with a sense of belonging and the reassurance that we are not alone. This chapter delves into the importance of building a community and fostering connections with individuals who share similar experiences. Through shared stories, compassionate listening, and the exchange of wisdom, we nurture our souls while finding the strength to face life's challenges head-on.

The Power of Shared Stories:

Human beings are natural storytellers, continually weaving the tapestry of our existence through narratives. In times of hardship, sharing our stories can be incredibly healing, both for ourselves and the listener. When we connect with others who are on a similar journey, their stories become a reflection of our own struggles and triumphs, amplifying the power of empathy and empathy we draw from our shared experiences.

Imagine a group of cancer survivors gathered in a small support circle. As each person recounts their journey through treatments, remission, and survivorship, the others listen intently, finding solace in knowing that their feelings are mirrored by someone else. Witnessing the narrative threads of resilience and courage, they not only gain newfound strength but also impart wisdom to their peers. While every story is unique, the common themes and emotions that arise provide comfort and inspiration, fostering a sense of community and camaraderie.

Compassionate Listening: An Act of Love:

Central to building authentic connections within a community is the art of compassionate listening. In a world often plagued by distractions and disconnected conversations, listening with an open heart and a genuine desire to understand is a rarity. Yet, when we extend this gift to others, it can bridge the gap of understanding and create bonds that withstand the test of time.

Listening with compassion requires more than physically being present; it demands active engagement, empathy, and the willingness to hold space for others' pain and joy. By creating an environment where vulnerability is met with genuine support and acceptance, we allow individuals on a similar journey to share their fears, doubts, and hopes freely. In doing so, we cultivate a safe haven for personal growth and transformation, where one's voice is heard, understood, and appreciated.

Through the exchange of our stories and attentive listening, we find the humanity that connects us all, fostering a deeper understanding of the shared struggles and triumphs we encounter throughout our lives. It is in these moments of collective vulnerability that we discover our strength lies not only within ourselves but in the support we find within our community.

Wisdom in the Exchange:

In the search for support from others on a similar journey, we often uncover a wealth of wisdom passed down through generations. This exchange of knowledge, insight, and guidance among individuals navigating shared experiences can be a beacon of hope, illuminating the path ahead.

A young parent attending a parenting support group, for instance, may feel overwhelmed and bewildered by the fullness of their responsibilities. However, upon engaging with more experienced parents who have already walked a similar path, they gain access to a treasure trove of wisdom. The seasoned parents share anecdotes, practical tips, and the assurance that these challenges are temporary, lifting the burden of doubt from the younger parent's shoulders.

Through the exchange of wisdom, we not only benefit from the experiences of others but also develop a sense of responsibility to pay it forward. This tacit contract within a supportive community compels each member to share their hard-earned knowledge, ensuring that the cycle of compassion and support continues for future generations.

Building a community and seeking support from others on a similar journey is an essential aspect of the human experience. In sharing our stories, listening with compassion, and exchanging wisdom, we nurture our souls and find solace in knowing that we are not alone in our struggles or joys. It is within these authentic connections that we discover the strength to face life's challenges head-on.

As you embark on your own journey, remember the importance of community and seek out those who can share in your triumphs, lend a listening ear during your darkest moments, and impart their hard-earned wisdom. The bonds you form within this supportive network will not only sustain you during difficult times but will also uplift your spirit and illuminate your path towards personal growth and fulfillment. Together, we can find strength, understanding, and a profound sense of belonging, paving the way for a brighter and more compassionate world.

Celebrating Heart's Triumphs: Recognizing and Honoring Progress in Relationships

Chapter 1: The Journey of Love

Love is an extraordinary emotion that has the power to transform lives. It takes us on a captivating and sometimes tumultuous journey, filled with ups and downs, joy and heartache. Relationships, whether romantic, familial, or platonic, form the intricate tapestry of our lives. They shape and mold us, bringing out both the best and worst in us. At times, it may feel overwhelming, but it is in recognizing and honoring the progress we have made in these relationships that we truly celebrate the triumph of the heart.

Chapter 2: Nurturing Self-Love

A healthy relationship begins with self-love. One cannot give what they do not have, and loving oneself is the foundation of loving others. It is imperative to recognize and celebrate the progress we have made in nurturing this self-love. This can be achieved through self-reflection, setting boundaries, and prioritizing self-care. When we acknowledge the growth we have experienced in these areas, we pave the way for deeper and more fulfilling connections with others.

Chapter 3: Building Trust

Trust is the cornerstone of any meaningful relationship. It takes time, patience, and effort to establish and maintain trust. As humans, we are flawed, and we may make mistakes that hurt those we love. However, it is in recognizing the progress we have made in rebuilding trust that we find the strength to move forward. Celebrating the triumphs in trust-building not only strengthens the bond between individuals but also fosters a sense of security and belonging.

Chapter 4: Communication and Understanding

Effective communication is key to any successful relationship. It requires active listening, empathy, and vulnerability. Celebrating the progress we have made in fostering open and honest communication allows us to grow individually and together. By recognizing the triumphs in understanding each other's needs, we create a safe space for dialogue, resolution, and deeper connections.

Chapter 5: Overcoming Challenges

Every relationship faces its share of challenges. From petty arguments to major disagreements, it is in recognizing and honoring the progress we have made in overcoming these obstacles that we find resilience and strength. By celebrating the triumphs in resilience, forgiveness, and compromise, we not only strengthen the relationship but also grow individually.

Chapter 6: Embracing Growth and Change

Relationships are living entities that require continuous growth and adaptation. As individuals, we evolve over time, and it is crucial to celebrate the progress we have made as we navigate these changes. Honoring the triumphs in embracing personal growth and supporting the growth of our loved ones fosters an environment of love, acceptance, and unity.

Chapter 7: Cultivating Appreciation and Gratitude

In the hustle and bustle of everyday life, it is easy to overlook the little things that make a relationship special. Yet, as human beings, we crave acknowledgment and appreciation. By recognizing and honoring the progress we have made in cultivating appreciation and gratitude, we infuse our relationships with positivity and love. Celebrating the triumphs in expressing gratitude and acknowledging the efforts of our loved ones strengthens the bonds we share.

Chapter 8: Celebrating Milestones

Every relationship reaches milestones – anniversaries, accomplishments, or simply moments of pure joy. These milestones are reminders of the journey we have undertaken together. By celebrating these triumphs, we infuse our relationships with joy, love, and a sense of accomplishment. Reflection on these milestones allows us to appreciate how far we have come and motivate us to continue growing together.

Chapter 9: The Power of Forgiveness

No relationship is perfect, and forgiveness is a vital component for its survival. It takes strength and humility to forgive, but it is in recognizing and honoring the progress we have made in practicing forgiveness that we celebrate the triumph of the heart. By letting go of grudges, resentments, and past hurts, we create space for healing, growth, and the deepening of our connections.

Chapter 10: Embracing Unconditional Love

Unconditional love is a rare gem that illuminates our relationships. It is the ability to love and cherish someone regardless of their flaws or shortcomings. By celebrating the triumphs in embracing this kind of love, we create a space where our relationships flourish. When we honor the progress we have made in showing unconditional love, we foster an environment where trust, understanding, and acceptance thrive.

Chapter 11: Cherishing the Present Moment

In a fast-paced world, we often forget to pause and cherish the present moment with our loved ones. It is in recognizing and honoring the progress we have made in being present that we celebrate the triumphs of the heart. By embracing the beauty of the moment, we create lasting memories and deepen our connections with those we hold dear.

Chapter 12: The Endless Journey

The journey of love is one that has no definitive end. It is a continuous process of growth, learning, and celebrating triumphs. Relationships are ever-evolving, and it is by recognizing and honoring the progress we have made that we find fulfillment and joy. Celebrating our triumphs in relationships allows us to appreciate the beauty of the human experience and truly honor the power of love.

As we close this chapter, it is important to remember that the celebration of our heart's triumphs requires conscious effort and perseverance. It is an ongoing journey that requires dedication to self-reflection, growth, and the nurturing of our relationships. So, let us continue to recognize and honor the progress we have made, cherishing every triumph and weaving a tapestry of love that withstands the test of time.

Chapter 8: Heart's External Influences: The Impact of the Environment

The human heart, an organ central to our existence, plays a vital role in maintaining our overall well-being. While we often associate heart health with factors such as diet and exercise, there is an underlying influence that we must not overlook—the impact of the environment. In this chapter, we will explore the various external influences on the heart and examine how our surroundings shape cardiovascular health.

1. Air Quality and Heart Health:

The quality of the air we breathe has a significant impact on our cardiovascular system. Pollutants such as particulate matter, ozone, and carbon monoxide can penetrate deep into our lungs, triggering inflammation and oxidative stress. These harmful effects have been linked to an increased risk of heart disease, heart attacks, and strokes. Research has shown that individuals living in areas with poor air quality are more likely to experience adverse cardiovascular events. As such, it is crucial to prioritize efforts to improve air pollution levels and reduce exposure to harmful airborne substances.

2. Noise Pollution and Cardiovascular Health:

The hustle and bustle of modern life often subject us to excessive noise levels, which can have detrimental effects on our heart health. Chronic exposure to noise pollution, whether from traffic, construction, or even loud music, has been associated with heightened risks of hypertension, myocardial infarction, and heart failure. The constant bombardment of noise disrupts our sleep patterns, increases stress levels, and elevates blood pressure, all of which place additional strain on the heart. Therefore, it is essential to create quieter environments and minimize our exposure to excessive noise whenever possible.

3. Green Spaces and Heart Health:

While the negative impacts of environmental factors may seem overwhelming, there is a silver lining—a natural solution lies within the beauty of green spaces. Research has consistently shown that living in close proximity to parks, forests, or green areas significantly improves heart health. Being in nature helps reduce stress, lower blood pressure, and enhance overall well-being. Engaging in activities like walking or exercising amidst greenery has shown immense benefits for cardiovascular health. Incorporating green spaces into urban planning and encouraging regular interaction with nature can be beneficial not only for our hearts but also for our mental and emotional well-being.

4. Climate Change and Cardiovascular Risk:

In recent years, the impacts of climate change have become increasingly evident. Rising temperatures, extreme weather events, and unpredictable climatic patterns have substantial consequences for our cardiovascular health. Heatwaves, for instance, pose a serious threat, as they can increase the risk of heart attacks and other cardiac events, especially among vulnerable populations. Additionally, climate-related events, such as hurricanes or floods, can lead to the displacement of individuals and communities, disrupting continuity of care and exacerbating heart health issues. As we grapple with the effects of climate change, it is imperative to implement strategies that both mitigate and adapt to these challenges, thereby safeguarding our cardiovascular well-being.

5. Socioeconomic Disparities and Heart Health:

The impact of the environment on heart health is not distributed equally across society. Socioeconomic disparities play a significant role in shaping the cardiovascular outcomes of individuals. Those living in impoverished areas often face limited access to healthy food options, safe recreational spaces, and adequate healthcare services. These factors, compounded by chronic stress and adversity, contribute to a higher burden of cardiovascular diseases in disadvantaged communities. Addressing these disparities requires a multifaceted approach, including equitable access to resources, education, and social support systems, which will help bridge the gap in heart health outcomes.

6. Built Environment and Heart Health:

The built environment, encompassing our neighborhoods, workplaces, and transportation systems, influences our daily behaviors and physical activity levels, which, in turn, impact heart health. Urban planning that promotes walkability, cycling infrastructure, and the creation of pedestrian-friendly spaces has proven beneficial for cardiovascular health. By designing environments that encourage physical activity, we can reduce the prevalence of sedentary lifestyles and associated cardiovascular risks.

7. Light Exposure and Circadian Rhythm:

The influence of the environment extends beyond our physical surroundings and also involves the regulation of our internal biological clock, known as the circadian rhythm. Exposure to natural light during the day and minimal light exposure at night play a crucial role in maintaining a healthy sleep-wake cycle. Disruptions to this rhythm, such as exposure to artificial light at night, can have adverse effects on our cardiovascular health, increasing the risk of conditions like hypertension and metabolic disorders. Understanding the impact of light on our bodies allows us to design environments that promote healthy circadian rhythms, benefiting heart health in the process.

The Digital Dilemma: How Social Media Affects Relationship Anxiety

The advent of social media has undoubtedly revolutionized the way we interact and connect with others. Platforms like Facebook, Instagram, and Snapchat have become integral parts of our lives, allowing us to share our experiences, thoughts, and emotions with a wider audience. Yet, with this digital revolution comes a downside – the impact of social media on relationship anxiety. In this chapter, we delve into the various ways in which social media exerts pressure on romantic relationships and exacerbates feelings of doubt, jealousy, and insecurity.

Social Media Comparison and the Fear of Missing Out (FOMO)

One of the primary reasons social media can spark relationship anxiety is the constant exposure to others' seemingly perfect lives and relationships. As individuals scroll through their feeds, they are bombarded with carefully curated posts, capturing blissful moments, luxurious vacations, and seemingly unbreakable connections. This phenomenon, known as social media comparison, can trigger feelings of inadequacy and self-doubt within relationships.

In a world where everyone appears to be living extraordinary lives, it is natural for individuals to question the state of their own relationships. They may find themselves wondering, "Are we happy enough? Are we adventurous enough? Are we as in love as they are?" Such comparisons often lead to unrealistic expectations and a constant fear of missing out on experiences that appear more exciting or fulfilling.

Mind Games: Jealousy and Social Media Stalking

Jealousy has long been recognized as a relationship killer, and social media provides the perfect breeding ground for its growth. Through platforms like Facebook and Instagram, individuals have access to personal information, photographs, and updates of their partner's connections, past and present. While this access can be harmless, scrolling through an ex-partner's vacation pictures or reading flirtatious comments on a partner's profile can quickly spiral into a web of doubt and insecurity.

The practice of social media stalking, though tempting, only serves to exacerbate jealousy and anxiety within relationships. Frequent monitoring of a partner's online activities may foster a sense of mistrust and paranoia, eroding the foundation of trust that is vital for a healthy relationship. This constant surveillance can also lead to misinterpretation of harmless interactions, creating unnecessary tension and conflicts.

The Highlight Reels and Emotional Well-being

Social media is often dubbed as the land of "highlight reels," where individuals predominantly share moments of joy, success, and happiness. However, this carefully crafted portrayal of one's life can have detrimental effects on both partners within a relationship. When individuals constantly witness the achievements and celebrations of their social media connections, it can lead to feelings of personal inadequacy, diminishing their own accomplishments. Consequently, those who constantly compare their lives to the often magnified versions they encounter on social media may experience heightened anxiety and lower self-esteem.

Furthermore, the relentless exposure to idealized versions of relationships on social media leads individuals to question the authenticity and satisfaction of their own partnerships. The pressure to live up to the airbrushed standards of Instagram-perfect romance can breed anxiety and despair. This comparison game can surface doubts about compatibility, intensifying anxiety and pushing individuals to constantly seek validation and reassurance from their partners.

Communication Breakdown: The Emoji Effect

While social media platforms have made communication convenient and instantaneous, their effects on intimate conversations can be detrimental. The adoption of emojis and abbreviated messages as substitutes for genuine expressions of emotion has become commonplace in online communication. This shift from nuanced in-person conversations to brief, emoji-laden text exchanges can hinder true emotional connections.

When important discussions are confined to 140-character tweets or series of hastily crafted Facebook messages, the richness and depth of genuine connection diminish. This limited form of communication can create misunderstandings, misinterpretations, and heightened anxiety, as partners struggle to decode the intended meaning behind an emoji-laden text. Such breakdowns in communication increase relationship anxiety, leaving partners feeling disconnected and unheard.

The digital era has undoubtedly reshaped the dynamics of intimate relationships, bringing both opportunities and challenges. We have explored the detrimental effects of social media on relationship anxiety, including the dangers of social media comparison, the growth of jealousy through stalking, the impact of highlight reels on emotional well-being, and the breakdown of genuine communication. By understanding these challenges, individuals can begin to navigate the digital landscape with caution, acknowledging the importance of maintaining realistic expectations and open lines of communication. As social media continues to evolve, we must adapt and establish healthy boundaries to ensure our relationships thrive in this ever-connected world.

Workplace Woes and the Heart: The Role of Career Stress in Relationship Strains

In today's fast-paced society, individuals often find themselves consumed by the demands and stresses of their careers. Long hours, tight deadlines, and high levels of competition can take a toll on one's physical and mental well-being, but what about their emotional well-being? What impact does career stress have on our relationships, particularly with our partners? This chapter explores the complex interplay between workplace woes and the heart, shedding light on the role of career stress in relationship strains.

The Modern Workforce:

Before diving into the effects of career stress on relationships, it is essential to understand the workings of the modern workforce. Over the past few decades, we have witnessed a significant shift in workplace dynamics and expectations. The line between work and personal life has become increasingly blurred, and individuals often find themselves bringing their professional pressures home. The constant connectivity provided by technology has made it difficult to disconnect and recharge, resulting in a continuous exposure to work-related stressors.

Impact on Emotional Well-being:

Career stress can have profound effects on an individual's emotional well-being. Feelings of exhaustion, anxiety, and disillusionment are common among those facing immense work pressures. This emotional strain often spills over into other areas of life, including personal relationships. When individuals are emotionally drained, it becomes challenging to meet the emotional needs of their partners, leading to communication breakdowns and conflicts within the relationship.

The Emotional Exhaustion-Relationship Connection:

One of the central components of career stress is emotional exhaustion. This sense of depletion is often a result of chronic job demands that exceed an individual's personal resources. When an individual is emotionally exhausted, they lack the emotional energy required to engage fully with their partner. This can lead to emotional detachment, decreased empathy, and reduced emotional support, all of which leave the partner feeling neglected and disconnected.

Work-Life Spillover:

The blurring boundaries between work and personal life can have significant repercussions on relationships. When work-related stress spills over into the home environment, it affects the quality of time spent together, eroding relationship satisfaction. Partners may feel neglected as their significant other consistently brings work-related worries and frustrations into their shared space. This work-life spillover, if left unaddressed, can cause resentment, increased conflict, and eventually lead to relationship dissatisfaction.

The Role of Work-Related Conflict:

Career stress can also manifest in the form of work-related conflict, such as inter-role conflict and work-family conflict. Inter-role conflict occurs when the demands of one role (e.g., career) interfere with the fulfillment of another role (e.g., spouse). This conflict can create tension, as individuals struggle to balance the competing demands and expectations placed upon them. Work-family conflict, on the other hand, arises when the pressures of work spill over into the family domain, making it difficult to maintain a harmonious relationship with a partner. Both inter-role conflict and work-family conflict have been found to be significant predictors of relationship strains and diminished satisfaction.

Coping Strategies:

While career stress is inherent in today's workplace, individuals can employ various strategies to mitigate its impact on their relationships. Firstly, engaging in open and honest communication with their partner about work-related stressors can help foster understanding and support. Sharing the burden allows for a shared sense of responsibility, making it easier to weather the storms together.

Additionally, setting boundaries between work and personal life is crucial. Designating specific times for work-related discussions and maintaining technology-free zones within the home creates space for quality time and relationship nurturing. Employing stress management techniques, such as exercise, meditation, or engaging in enjoyable activities, can also help individuals unwind and recharge, enabling them to be more present and engaged in their relationships.

Supporting One Another:

Support from a partner plays a crucial role in managing career stress and its impact on relationships. Partners who offer emotional support, understanding, and encouragement can significantly buffer the negative effects of workplace stressors. By being available to listen, providing a safe space for venting, and offering reassurance during difficult times, partners become invaluable allies in battling workplace woes.

Societal Echoes: The Impact of Current Events on Relationship Dynamics

In our rapidly evolving world, where information travels at the speed of light and global events shape our daily lives, it is no surprise that these external forces have a profound impact on the dynamics of our relationships. From political unrest to economic crises, from pandemics to social movements, current events serve as a backdrop against which our personal interactions unfold. This chapter explores the intricate interplay between societal events and the relationships we develop, exploring how they influence various aspects such as communication, trust, conflict, and even the formation and dissolution of partnerships.

The Ripple Effect of Communication:

One of the most immediate effects of current events on relationships is evident in the realm of communication. When major events unfold, conversations about politics, social issues, and cultural changes dominate our collective discourse. Individuals often find themselves aligning with different viewpoints, leading to heated debates and sometimes even conflict within relationships.

Take, for example, a couple navigating a period of political tension in their country. As election season rolls around, one partner may become deeply invested in a particular candidate or party, while the other may hold opposing views. This ideological divide can ignite clashes in conversations, challenging the harmony that once existed. The exchange of differing opinions can lead to emotional labor, triggering the need for open-mindedness, empathy, and active listening within relationships.

Trust in Times of Turmoil:

Current events can also have a profound impact on trust within relationships. During times of crisis, individuals often seek solace and support in their partners. However, societal events can also create doubt and uncertainty, affecting the level of trust in the relationship.

For instance, consider the impact of economic downturns on relationships. When financial stability is threatened, people may experience heightened levels of stress and anxiety. Economic hardships may lead to job losses, financial insecurity, and a general sense of unpredictability. In such times, individuals may question their partner's ability to provide and protect, leading to strained trust dynamics. Encouraging open and transparent communication, practicing empathy, and providing reassurance are all crucial in rebuilding and maintaining trust during times of turmoil.

Conflict Resolutions in the Face of Crisis:

The diverse range of societal events often sparks heated debates, fueling potential conflicts within relationships. Whether it be social movements, controversial policies, or even global health emergencies, the clash of opinions within partnerships can strain the very foundation of a relationship.

Consider a couple who holds contrasting views on a social movement such as gender equality. One partner believes in the importance of equity and advocates for equal rights, while the other is skeptical of the movement's impact. Engaging in such conversations requires emotional intelligence, patience, and respect for one another's perspectives. Successfully navigating these conflicts involves actively listening, seeking common ground, and validating each other's experiences.

Formation and Dissolution of Partnerships:

Current events can also influence the formation and dissolution of relationships. Major societal shifts often lead individuals to reassess their values, priorities, and aspirations, subsequently impacting their choice of partners.

For example, during times of social awakening, such as the #MeToo movement, individuals may become more aware of power dynamics, misogyny, and issues related to consent. This heightened consciousness can prompt a reevaluation of existing relationships, leading some individuals to seek partners who share similar values and actively support gender equality. Conversely, it may also lead to the dissolution of relationships when individuals realize fundamental disparities in their beliefs and actions.

As our world continues to evolve, the impact of societal events on relationship dynamics will remain an integral aspect of our human experience. Understanding and navigating these influences is essential to nurture healthy, lasting relationships. By being conscious of the ripple effects that external forces can have on our personal lives, we can foster dialogue, enhance empathy, and promote growth within our relationships. Moreover, it is imperative to recognize that despite the challenges these events pose, they also provide opportunities for personal and relational transformation if approached with openness, empathy, and a willingness to learn and understand differing perspectives.

Friendships and the Heart: Navigating Peer Influence in Romantic Relationships

Friendships have always played a crucial role in our lives, shaping our personalities, influencing our decisions, and providing emotional support. They are an integral part of the human experience, and when it comes to romantic relationships, friendships can have a significant impact. In this chapter, we will explore the intricate dynamics between our friendships and romantic relationships, focusing on how peer influence can shape our romantic decisions and interactions. We will dive into the fascinating world of friend groups, social circles, and the intricate web of advice, opinions, and expectations that come along with them. So, let us embark on this journey of understanding and unraveling the complexities of friendships and their effect on matters of the heart.

Friend Groups as a Crucible of Advice and Influence:

Friend groups often serve as testing grounds for our relationships, where ideas, opinions, and advice are freely shared. They can provide invaluable guidance and perspectives but can also be a source of confusion and conflict. As we navigate the treacherous waters of romantic relationships, it is essential to understand the role our friends play in shaping our decisions.

Influence, Comparisons, and Unspoken Expectations:

Within our friend groups, we can't help but observe and compare our own relationships with those of our friends. We might find ourselves questioning whether our relationship is as fulfilling, exciting, or "perfect" as theirs. These comparisons can spark feelings of inadequacy or FOMO (fear of missing out), leading to doubt and insecurity. Managing these unspoken expectations is crucial to ensure the health and longevity of our romantic relationships.

The Perils of Unsolicited Advice:

Though our friends' advice might be well-intentioned, it is vital to recognize that what works for one couple may not work for another. Unsolicited advice can sometimes do more harm than good, causing unnecessary conflict or doubt. Learning how to sift through the advice received and evaluating its relevance to our unique circumstances becomes necessary to make informed decisions for our own relationships.

Nurturing Healthy Boundaries:

Boundaries are essential in any relationship, and the same holds for our friendships as they intersect with our romantic partnerships. We must learn to create and communicate healthy boundaries with our friends concerning our romantic relationships. Open dialogue, mutual understanding, and respect are key in ensuring that our friends' influence remains positive while allowing us the freedom to make autonomous choices.

Peer Pressure and Decision Making:

Peer pressure is a powerful force that can significantly impact our choices in romantic relationships. Whether it be conforming to societal expectations, following the advice of influential friends, or giving in to the fear of missing out, peer pressure can lead us astray from our true desires and needs. Recognizing the signs of peer pressure and understanding its impact on decision-making can help us preserve our authenticity and make choices aligned with our own values.

Maintaining Individuality within Relationships:

In the pursuit of a romantic partnership, it is essential to retain our individuality and not lose ourselves in the process. The influence of friends can sometimes blur the lines between where our own desires end and those of our partner or friend group begin. Navigating this delicate balance requires self-awareness, effective communication, and the courage to assert our needs and desires within our relationships.

Challenging Gender Stereotypes and Expectations:

Friendships and peer influence can also shape our perceptions of gender roles, which may influence our romantic relationships. Challenging societal stereotypes and expectations is crucial to promoting equality and fostering healthy dynamics within our partnerships. By breaking free from traditional gender norms, we can create relationships that celebrate individuality, respect, and shared responsibilities.

As we conclude this chapter, we have explored the profound relationship between friendships and romantic partnerships. We have deep-dived into the dynamic social circles that can both support and challenge our relationships. It is important to recognize the power of peer influence and how it can shape our decisions, assumptions, and expectations. By nurturing healthy boundaries, asserting our individuality, and challenging societal norms, we can navigate the complex web of friendships and romantic relationships with confidence and grace. Remember, each relationship is unique, and while the opinions of our friends can be invaluable, ultimately, we hold the power to make choices that align with our hearts and pave the way for genuine happiness.

Chapter 9: The Heart's Path to Self-Care and Personal Growth

In a fast-paced, interconnected world, where demands and responsibilities seem never-ending, it is crucial to pause and reflect on our own well-being. Each one of us has an innate longing for personal growth and a desire to lead fulfilling lives. This chapter explores the heart's path to self-care and personal growth, delving into the importance of nurturing ourselves, developing healthy relationships, and embracing vulnerability as a catalyst for growth. By embarking on this transformative journey, you can uncover your true potential, cultivate self-compassion, and ultimately find lasting happiness and fulfillment.

Embracing Self-Care:

Self-care is often misunderstood as a luxury or indulgence. However, it is, in fact, an essential component of our overall well-being. Nurturing ourselves requires turning inward, listening to our needs, and creating space for activities that restore and energize us. It encompasses practices such as mindfulness, journaling, and engaging in activities that bring joy and purpose to our lives. By prioritizing self-care, we can nourish our minds, bodies, and souls, which in turn enhances our mental and emotional resilience.

Understanding Boundaries:

A key aspect of self-care is setting and maintaining healthy boundaries. Boundaries are the invisible lines that establish limits and define what is acceptable behavior from others in our lives. By communicating these boundaries clearly, we create space for healthy relationships to thrive while protecting our own emotional well-being. Understanding that it is okay to say no, asking for help when needed, and having honest conversations about our needs fosters a sense of empowerment and self-respect.

Cultivating Healthy Relationships:

As social beings, cultivating healthy relationships is intrinsic to our personal growth. Surrounding ourselves with supportive, positive individuals who share our values and goals can greatly influence our overall well-being. Meaningful connections provide a safe space for vulnerability, authenticity, and continuous learning. Intentionally investing time and energy in nurturing relationships builds a strong foundation for our personal growth journey.

Embracing Vulnerability:

Although often seen as a weakness, vulnerability is a crucial catalyst for personal growth. It is through our vulnerabilities that we connect with others on a deeper level, fostering empathy, compassion, and understanding. By embracing vulnerability, we open ourselves up to new experiences, insights, and personal transformations. It takes courage to expose our true selves, but in doing so, we give ourselves permission to let go of pretenses and embrace our authentic selves, leading to personal growth and self-acceptance.

Practicing Mindfulness:

In our chaotic and fast-paced lives, it is essential to cultivate mindfulness - the practice of being present and fully engaged in the current moment. This mindfulness allows us to step away from our racing thoughts and ground ourselves in the reality of the present. Through mindfulness practices such as meditation, deep breathing, and self-reflection, we can gain clarity, reduce stress, and unlock our inner wisdom. Mindfulness also enables us to cultivate gratitude, appreciating the small joys and blessings that surround us.

The Power of Intention:

Intentionality is a powerful tool for fostering personal growth. It involves setting clear intentions, aligning our actions with our values, and consciously working towards our goals. By identifying what truly matters to us, we can create a roadmap for personal growth and self-improvement. Setting intentions provides direction and motivation, allowing us to make intentional choices that align with our personal values, and ultimately, leading us to a more fulfilling and purposeful life.

The Role of Self-Compassion:

Self-compassion is the act of treating ourselves with kindness, understanding, and forgiveness, especially in times of difficulty or failure. It involves acknowledging our imperfections and offering ourselves the same empathy and support we would extend to a loved one. Cultivating self-compassion allows us to let go of self-judgment and embrace self-acceptance, creating a nurturing environment for personal growth. This practice also enhances our ability to bounce back from setbacks, as we learn to view them as valuable learning experiences rather than personal failures.

Embarking on the heart's path to self-care and personal growth is a transformative journey of self-discovery and self-actualization. By embracing self-care, understanding the importance of boundaries, cultivating healthy relationships, embracing vulnerability, practicing mindfulness, setting intentions, and cultivating self-compassion, we can unlock our true potential and create a life that is aligned with our authentic selves. This journey is not linear, but rather a continuous process of growth, self-reflection, and adaptation. By taking small, intentional steps, we can create a ripple effect that positively influences every aspect of our lives. So, let us embrace this path with an open heart and an eagerness to explore the uncharted territories of our souls.

Solo Sojourns: The Importance of Alone Time in Alleviating Relationship Anxiety

In the hustle and bustle of modern life, it is easy to become overwhelmed by the demands of work, family, and relationships. We often find ourselves constantly surrounded by others, leaving little time for self-reflection and personal growth. However, contrary to popular belief, spending time alone can have incredible benefits for our mental well-being, especially in the context of romantic relationships. In this chapter, we will explore the concept of solo sojourns and delve into why carving out alone time is essential for alleviating relationship anxiety and maintaining a healthy and fulfilling love life.

Understanding Relationship Anxiety:

Before delving into the significance of solo sojourns, it is important to comprehend the nature of relationship anxiety. Many individuals experience doubts and insecurities within their romantic partnerships, often stemming from fear of rejection, abandonment, or simply a lack of self-confidence. These anxieties can manifest as jealousy, possessiveness, or even a constant need for reassurance from our partners. While these feelings are a natural part of being in a relationship, if left unchecked, they can lead to resentment, frustration, and eventual relationship breakdown.

Recognizing the Role of Alone Time:

Solitude is often mistaken as a sign of isolation or loneliness, but it is, in fact, a state of self-reflection and introspection. Taking time for ourselves allows us to reconnect with our true selves, rediscover our passions, and gain a clearer perspective on our relationships. It is during these moments of solitude that we can examine our fears, anxieties, and insecurities without external influences, enabling personal growth and increased self-awareness.

Understanding Personal Boundaries:

One of the main reasons why solo sojourns are essential for alleviating relationship anxiety lies in the establishment and maintenance of personal boundaries. In any healthy relationship, it is crucial to have a balance between individuality and togetherness. Spending regular time alone helps define personal boundaries and fosters a sense of independence, reducing the reliance on our partners for our happiness and emotional well-being. By understanding and respecting our own boundaries, we can communicate them effectively to our partners, leading to a healthier and more fulfilling relationship dynamic.

Regaining Personal Identity:

When we become deeply entangled in our relationships, it is easy to lose sight of our own individual identity. We may prioritize our partner's needs and desires over our own or find ourselves compromising on our own values and interests. Engaging in solo sojourns allows us to rediscover our personal passions, interests, and desires. By investing time in ourselves, we can rejuvenate our personal identity, bring a renewed sense of self to our relationship, and contribute meaningfully to the partnership.

Enhancing Communication and Emotional Intimacy:

Alone time not only allows us to reconnect with ourselves but also enhances our ability to communicate effectively within our relationships. By exploring our own thoughts and emotions independently, we become more skilled at articulating our needs, fears, and desires to our partners. This increased self-awareness leads to improved emotional intimacy, as we can express ourselves openly and honestly, fostering a deeper connection with our loved ones.

Building Self-Confidence:

Solo sojourns provide us the opportunity to develop a sense of self-confidence and self-assurance. Engaging in activities alone allows us to confront and conquer our fears, step outside of our comfort zone, and build resilience. As we grow in confidence, our relationship anxiety diminishes, and we become better equipped to handle challenges that may arise within our partnerships. Ultimately, this newfound self-assurance benefits both ourselves and our relationships.

Embracing Solitude for Mindfulness:

Solitude can be a powerful tool for practicing mindfulness and self-care. In our modern, hyperconnected world, we seldom have the chance to unplug and focus solely on ourselves. By engaging in meditative activities, journaling, or partaking in hobbies that bring us joy, we can reduce stress, anxiety, and relationship pressures. These moments of peace allow us to recharge, reflect, and approach our relationships with a renewed sense of purpose and positivity.

Solo sojourns are not a selfish or neglectful act; they are an essential part of maintaining a healthy and fulfilling relationship. By embracing moments of solitude, we enhance our self-awareness, establish personal boundaries, regain our personal identity, and foster effective communication within our partnerships. Embracing alone time and practicing self-care not only alleviates relationship anxiety but also cultivates a stronger, more resilient love life. May we all recognize the significance of solo sojourns and embrace these moments of personal growth and self-reflection in our journey towards happier, more fulfilling relationships.

Growth Beyond the Heart: Personal Development and Its Impact on Relationships

In the journey of life, personal development stands as the compass that guides us towards self-discovery, growth, and fulfillment. But what is often overlooked is the profound impact it has on our relationships. As we embark on the path of personal growth, we inherently transform ourselves, reshape our worldview, and effectively ripple these changes into every connection we forge. This chapter aims to explore the intricate relationship between personal development and our connections with others, shedding light on how cultivating ourselves ultimately leads to more meaningful and fulfilling relationships.

Understanding Personal Development

Before delving into the influence of personal development on our relationships, it is crucial to grasp the essence of this transformative process. Personal development encompasses a multidimensional approach towards self-improvement, where individuals intentionally work towards expanding their knowledge, honing their skills, and nurturing their emotional, mental, and spiritual well-being. It involves self-reflection, setting goals, and taking deliberate actions to unlock one's true potential. At its core, personal development is not limited to the acquisition of external achievements but also encompasses the growth of our character and values.

The Transformational Power of Personal Development

When we embark on a journey of personal growth, we embark on a journey of self-discovery and transformation. As we delve deeper into understanding our values, passions, and fears, we gain invaluable insights into ourselves. This self-awareness is a cornerstone of healthy relationships, as it allows us to communicate our needs, boundaries, and desires more effectively. When we know ourselves better, we can show up as more authentic and genuine individuals, facilitating deeper connections with others.

Furthermore, personal development enhances our emotional intelligence. As we learn to navigate our own emotions, we become more adept at empathizing and understanding the emotions of those around us. This heightened emotional intelligence cultivates deeper connections, as we become better equipped to support others in their own journeys. It allows us to foster more compassionate and empathetic relationships, where trust and understanding thrive.

Self-Confidence and Its Impact on Relationships

Personal development goes hand in hand with building self-confidence. As we break free from self-limiting beliefs and inner obstacles, we unleash untapped potential within ourselves. This newfound self-confidence radiates into our relationships, impacting them positively. When we believe in ourselves, we become more courageous in expressing our authentic selves, standing up for our needs, and pursuing our aspirations. This self-assuredness creates a more balanced dynamic in relationships, preventing the erosion of one's individuality and fostering a sense of equality.

Moreover, self-confidence permits us to embrace vulnerability. It is through vulnerability that we invite others to reciprocate trust and openness. Personal development allows us to feel more comfortable being vulnerable, as we understand that it is through vulnerability that we cultivate the most intimate and genuine connections. By embracing vulnerability and letting our walls down, we invite others to do the same, deepening the bonds we share.

Resilience and Adaptability in Relationships

Life is an ever-evolving journey, and personal development equips us with the resilience and adaptability needed to navigate its complexities. As we grow personally, we develop a greater capacity to handle life's challenges and setbacks. This resilience not only serves us individually but also strengthens our relationships. When both partners in a relationship are committed to personal growth, they can weather storms with greater emotional fortitude. Personal development equips individuals with the tools to communicate effectively, manage conflicts constructively, and support each other during difficult times.

Furthermore, personal growth facilitates adaptability, allowing individuals to embrace change and uncertainty. In relationships, adaptability becomes crucial in navigating the ebb and flow of life together. When we prioritize our own personal development, we become more open to change, less resistant to the unknown, and more willing to embrace growth within our relationships. This flexibility and adaptability enable relationships to thrive amidst life's unpredictable challenges.

Cultivating Shared Values and Goals

One of the remarkable aspects of personal development is the clarity it brings to our values and goals. As we continuously refine our personal values and set meaningful goals, we inadvertently influence our relationships. Personal development encourages us to engage in self-reflection and align our values and goals with those of our partner. This alignment allows for a more harmonious and fulfilling partnership, fostering shared aspirations and mutual growth.

Moreover, the pursuit of personal development inspires those around us, catalyzing their own transformative journeys. As we exemplify growth and resilience, our relationships become breeding grounds for growth, and our partners become inspired to embark on their own paths of personal development. In this way, personal growth becomes a catalyst for expanding not only our own lives but also the lives of those we love.

Personal development is an extraordinary journey of self-discovery, growth, and transformation. As we commit to cultivating ourselves, we inevitably create a ripple effect that extends beyond our own hearts, profoundly impacting our relationships. By better understanding ourselves, nurturing self-confidence, embracing vulnerability, developing resilience, and aligning our values and goals with those we love, we foster deeper connections and more fulfilling relationships. This chapter has explored the profound synergy between personal development and relationships, emphasizing the indispensability of self-growth in our pursuit of love, fulfillment, and deep emotional connectedness.

Physical Vitality, Emotional Stability: The Link between Physical Health and Relationship Wellness

In today's fast-paced world, maintaining a healthy and thriving relationship can seem like an uphill battle. Juggling work commitments, financial pressures, and personal responsibilities can leave little time or energy for nurturing our most important relationships. However, what many individuals fail to realize is that their physical health plays a significant role in the overall well-being of their relationships. In this chapter, we will delve into the intricate connection between physical vitality and emotional stability and explore how investing in our health can lead to flourishing relationships.

Understanding the Mind-Body Connection

The mind-body connection is a fundamental concept that links physical health and emotional well-being. Numerous studies have found an intricate and reciprocal relationship between our physical and mental states. It is through this lens that we can begin to comprehend how our physical vitality directly impacts our ability to maintain satisfying and lasting relationships.

Physical Health Impacts Emotional Stability

1. Energy Levels

One of the most noticeable effects of poor physical health on our relationships is the depletion of energy levels. When our bodies are fatigued, it becomes exceptionally challenging to engage and connect with our partners emotionally. Simple tasks can feel overwhelming, and our ability to provide the necessary emotional support to our loved ones diminishes. On the other hand, investing in our physical health by exercising regularly, getting enough sleep, and consuming a balanced diet boosts our energy levels, fostering emotional stability within our relationships.

2. Stress Management

Stress is an inevitable part of life, and how we handle it can significantly impact our relationships. When we neglect our physical health, stress levels tend to rise. Higher stress levels can manifest as irritability, anger, and impatience, which can strain even the strongest of relationships. However, engaging in regular physical activity, practicing mindfulness techniques, and adopting a healthy lifestyle can help manage stress effectively. By doing so, we create a more stable and supportive environment for our partners.

3. Emotional Regulation

Emotional regulation is crucial for maintaining healthy relationships, as it allows us to respond to our partners in a calm and rational manner. Physical health directly impacts our ability to regulate our emotions. Individuals who neglect their physical well-being are more likely to experience mood swings, heightened emotional reactivity, and difficulty managing conflicts. Conversely, regular exercise and a healthy diet are known to positively influence our brain chemistry, providing us with better emotional control.

Relationship Wellness Enhances Physical Health

While physical health contributes to emotional stability, it is essential to understand that relationship wellness also has a reciprocal effect on our physical well-being.

1. Social Support

A strong and fulfilling relationship can provide a vital support system that positively impacts our physical health. Research has consistently shown that individuals in satisfying relationships have lower levels of stress hormones, improved immune responses, and reduced risk of cardiovascular diseases. Moreover, having a supportive partner motivates and encourages us to prioritize our physical health, leading to positive lifestyle changes and healthier habits.

2. Shared Activities

Engaging in shared activities is not only an excellent way to strengthen a relationship but also a stepping stone towards improved physical health. Couples that participate in physical activities together, such as hiking, biking, or attending exercise classes, foster a sense of companionship and teamwork. Additionally, it promotes a healthier lifestyle for both partners, leading to enhanced physical vitality for both individuals.

3. Emotional Well-being

A healthy and fulfilling relationship provides emotional security and stability, which directly correlates with improved physical health. When we feel loved, supported, and understood by our partners, our bodies respond by releasing hormones that reduce stress and boost the immune system. This emotional well-being contributes to overall physical vitality, as our bodies are better equipped to fight off illnesses and maintain optimal health.

Practical Tips for Achieving Physical Vitality and Emotional Stability

Now that we understand the intricate link between physical health and relationship wellness, let's explore some practical tips for achieving both.

1. Open Communication

Develop open and honest communication with your partner to understand each other's physical and emotional needs. Talk about your respective health goals and how you can support each other in achieving them. By communicating openly, you create a safe and nurturing environment that promotes both physical and emotional well-being.

2. Make Time for Each Other

In today's busy world, it is crucial to carve out dedicated quality time for your relationship. Schedule regular date nights or engage in activities you both enjoy. By making time for each other, you strengthen the emotional bond and create opportunities to prioritize your physical health as a couple.

3. Prioritize Self-Care

Remember that your physical health is your responsibility. Prioritize self-care by engaging in regular exercise, establishing a healthy sleep routine, and nourishing your body with nutritious foods. By taking care of yourself, you set an example for your partner and inspire them to do the same.

4. Seek Professional Help if Needed

If you are struggling with physical health issues or emotional instability, do not hesitate to seek professional help. A qualified healthcare provider or therapist can provide valuable guidance and support in navigating these challenges, both on an individual and relationship level.

Physical vitality and emotional stability are critical components for maintaining a healthy and thriving relationship. By recognizing and investing in the link between physical health and relationship wellness, we open doors to a fulfilling and joyful partnership. Remember, taking care of your physical health not only benefits yourself but also enhances the well-being of your loved ones. Start today by incorporating small changes that cultivate physical vitality and emotional stability, and watch your relationship flourish.